THE BOOK OF Divination

A guide to predicting the future

Michael Johnstone

All images courtesy of Shutterstock.

This edition published in 2023 by Sirius Publishing, a division of
Arcturus Publishing Limited,
26/27 Bickels Yard, 151–153 Bermondsey Street,
London SE1 3HA

ISBN: 978-1-3988-2759-2
AD011032US

Printed in China

Contents

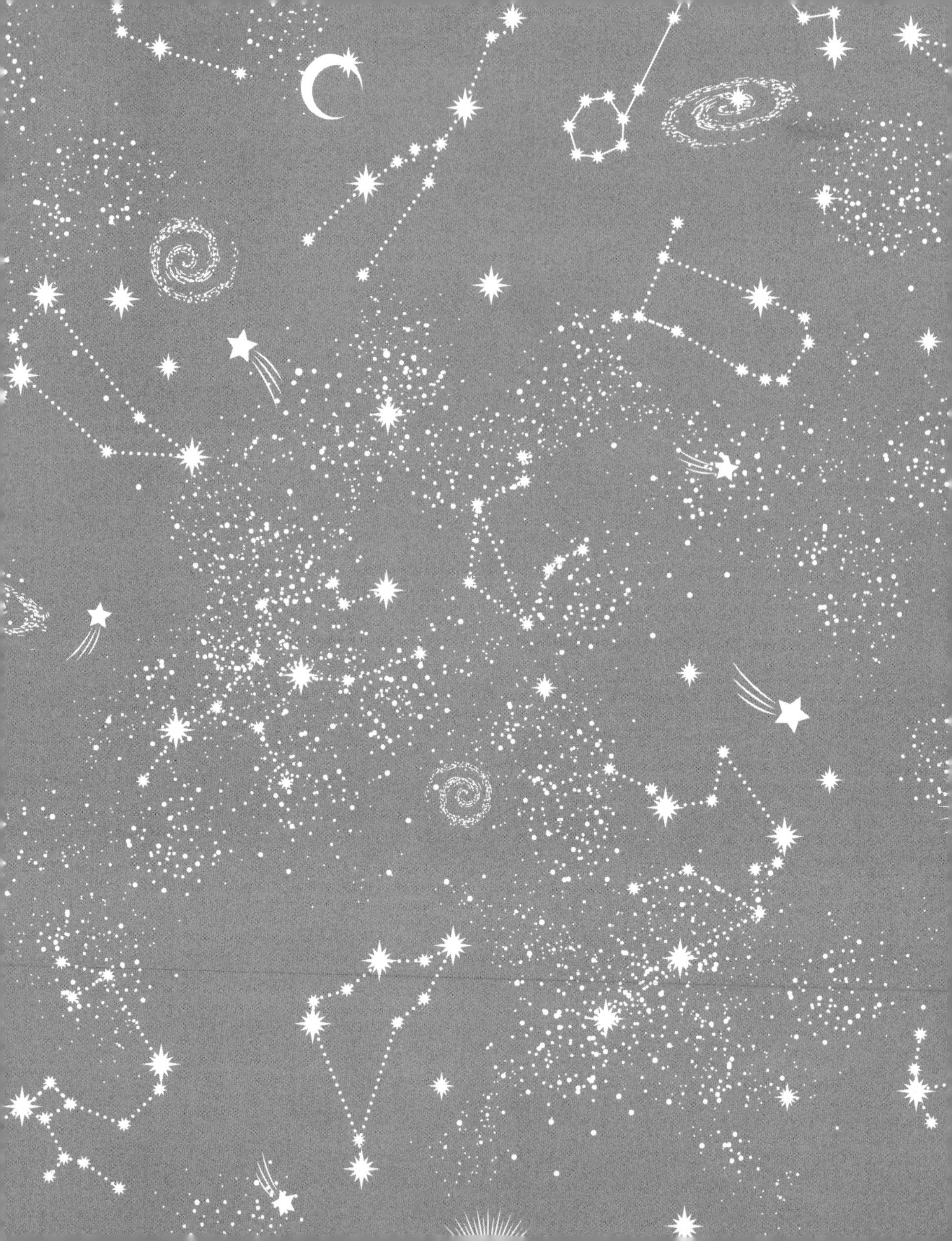

Introduction

Most of us attempt to foretell the future on a daily basis, although we may not think of it like that. From the stock broker who tries to predict the market to the grocer who tries to foresee what customers will buy, we are all amateur soothsayers. However, we also wish we could predict the future in less prosaic areas of life. When will we meet our great love? Which career should we pursue? If only we had a crystal ball to peer into and discover the answers. Well, we do!

You can use the techniques in this book to discover what will happen in your life through traditional methods of divination such as runes, palmistry, or even gazing into that crystal ball we just mentioned.

Our contributors include Michael Johnstone, who teaches you how decipher tea leaves as well as use crystals, the I Ching, Chinese astrology, numerology, palmistry and runes. And Pamela Ball gives us her guide to prophetic and magical dreaming.

In short, if you need to divine anything, you hold in your hands the guide to help you do it.

WHAT IS DIVINATION?

Divination is:

1. The action or practice of divining; the foretelling of future events or discovery of what is hidden or obscure by supernatural or magical means. Also, with a [article] and pl. [plural] an exercise of this, a prophecy, an augury.
2. Successful conjecture or guessing.

What the dictionary definitions fail to do is give any hint of the breadth of the ways in which the action of divining can be practiced.

What follows is partial list of practices compiled by an organization called BoxArt, reproduced here with its generous permission. We have edited and abridged it for this edition.

AEROMANCY

Aeromancy looks at cloud shapes, comets and other phenomena not normally visible in the heavens (see also Meteoromancy).

ALEUROMANCY

Anyone who has eaten a fortune cookie has indulged in aleuromancy, whereby answers to questions are rolled into balls of dough that, once baked, are chosen at random by those who have questions.

ALOMANCY

Also known as halomancy, alomancy involves studying the patterns made by table salt poured from the hand of the practitioner onto a consecrated surface or small area of land, preferably one used only for divination.

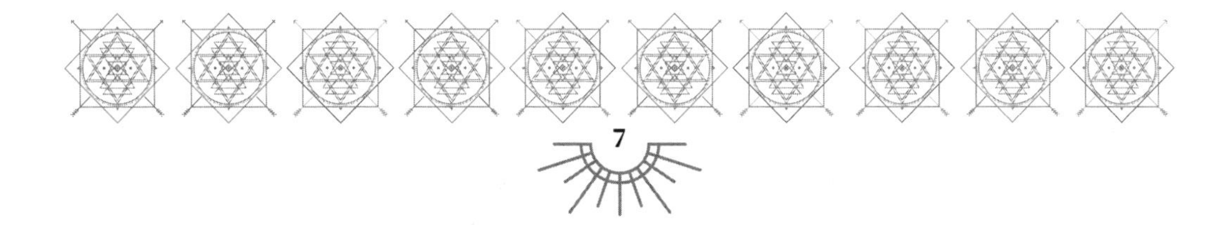

ALPHITOMANCY

Specially baked cakes are fed to those who stand accused of a misdeed of some sort, to establish guilt or innocence. The cakes are digestible by someone with a clear conscience, but are unpleasant to the guilty.

APANTOMANCY

A chance meeting with animals such as black cats, many types of birds, and other creatures is believed by some to be a sign of things to come.

ASTRAGLOMANCY

Sometimes known as astragyromancy, this method of divination uses special dice that bear numbers and letters.

ASTROLOGY

Those who practice astrology look at the Sun, the Moon, the planets and the stars, and their position and passage through the sky.

BIBLIOMANCY

In this practice, a question is asked, a book is opened at random, and the words on which the eye first falls are interpreted for the answer.

BOTANOMANCY

Botanomancers look at the shapes made in wood and leaf fires to discern future events.

CAPNOMANCY

Capnomancy concerns itself with interpreting the forms taken by smoke from a fire.

CARTOMANCY

Competing with astrology for the No. 1 spot in the top twenty of divination (in the West at least), cartomancy uses cards to answer questions. The cards may be from an ordinary pack or a special one, such as the Tarot.

CAUSIOMANCY

Causiomancers gaze at burning objects and draw conclusions from the way they react to the heat.

CERAUNOMANCY

Many ancient peoples believed that thunder and lightning were one of the ways in which the gods communicated with each other. What better way to divine the future than to eavesdrop on their conversations?

CEROMANCY

Also known as ceroscopy, ceromancy practitioners pour molten wax into water and analyze the resulting shapes.

CHIROMANCY

Closely allied to palmistry (see below), chiromancy concerns itself only with the lines of the hands, whereas palmistry uses other features of the hand.

CHIROGNOMY

Like palmistry (see below), chirognomy also looks at the hands. Chirognomancers study their general formation rather than the aspects considered by chiromancers and palmists.

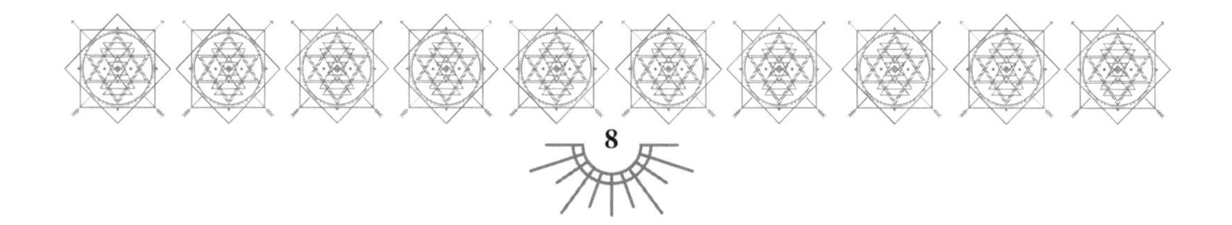

CLAIRAUDIENCE
The word means "clear hearing." This method of divination is usually regarded as a form of extrasensory perception (ESP), whereby unseen spirits who inhabit the future "speak" to those who have "the gift."

CLAIRVOYANCE
Using this form of ESP, clairvoyants "see" into the future, either in a self-induced trance during which images come to mind, or in flashes that can come, unsettlingly, out of the blue.

CLEROMANCY
Cleromancers look at the shifting patterns of seashells and pebbles on the beach that have either been moved by the tide or taken from a beach and dropped from the hands of the diviner. Another method of cleromancy is to hold a seashell up to the ear.

CLIDOMANCY
Also known as cleidomancy, clidomancy interprets the twistings and twirlings of a key suspended from a specially blessed or charmed cord (see also Radiesthesia).

COSCINOMANCY
Whereas clidomancers use a key, coscinomancers use a suspended sieve for divination (see also Radiesthesia).

CRYSTALLOMANCY
Crystallomancers need not use a crystal ball; any crystal can work.

DACTYLOMANCY
This is a branch of radiesthesia (see below) that uses a ring suspended on a piece of string or consecrated cord.

DAPHNOMANCY
People who divine using daphnomancy burn laurel branches on an open fire and interpret the crackling that fills the air.

DENDROMANCY
Like daphnomancy (see above), wood is the key to this method of divination—in this case oak or mistletoe.

DOWSING
In dowsing, water or precious metal is divined by using a forked rod that vibrates when held over the spot where what is being searched for is to be found. Hazel is the favored wood for the purpose.

GENETHIALOGY
This is the branch of astrology that predicts the path a person's life will take by plotting the positions of the stars and planets in the various astrological houses at the time of birth.

GRAPHOLOGY
Handwriting has long been held to provide a key to character analysis. Indeed, some firms have such a strong belief in graphology that they will not offer employment to anyone whose handwriting does not pass the test.

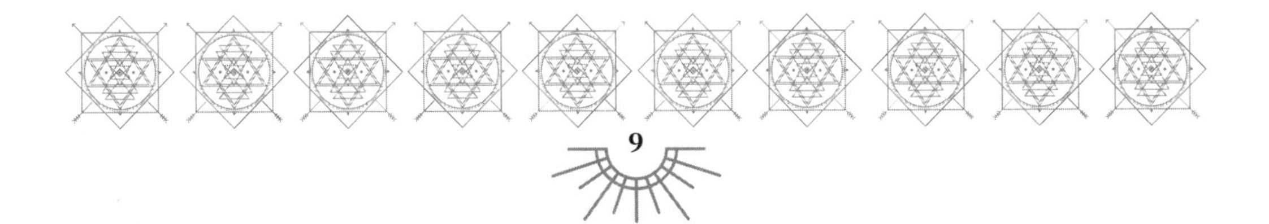

HOROSCOPY
This is more or less another name for astrology.

HYDROMANCY
Water—its color, ebb and flow, and the ripples produced by pebbles dropped in a pool—is the inspiration behind this form of divination.

LAMPADOMANCY
In this practice, the flickering flame of a special torch can shed light on the future.

LECANOMANCY
Lecanomancers gaze into a basin of water in much the same way that crystallomancers (see above) focus on crystals, hoping that as they reflect on their own or their followers' questions, answers will be revealed.

LIBANOMANCY
Libanomancers observe and interpret the smoke and ash produced by burning incense.

LITHOMANCY
Precious gems have long fascinated humankind; it is no surprise, therefore, to learn that they are used in divination.

MARGARITOMANCY
Margaritomancers hold a pearl in their hands, think deeply of the questions they want answered, and drop it onto a solid surface. The way it bounces, rolls, and comes to rest provides insights into the future.

METAGNOMY
Many seers fall into a trance during which they have visions of the future. Sometimes clairvoyants do this, as do practitioners of other kinds of divination. Metagnomy is a general term for this divination.

METEOROMANCY
Meteoromancers believe meteors and shooting stars can illumine the future.

NUMEROLOGY
Numerology divines by interpreting numbers, dates and the numerical value of letters.

OENOMANCY
Oenomancers believe that gazing at wine poured into special chalices will foretell events. The wine can also be poured out of a chalice, and the patterns it forms yield clues.

ONEIROMANCY
Oneiromancy, the interpretation of dreams, is one of the oldest forms of divination.

ONOMANCY
Onomancy has its roots in numerology (see above). The letters and syllables formed by a name are ascribed values that combine to enable the seer to plot a course of action.

ONYCHOMANCY
This branch of palmistry (see below) focuses on the fingernails—their shape, length, and other features—rather than the whole hand.

OOMANTIA
Oomantia (also known as ooscopy and ovamancy), is a method of divination that

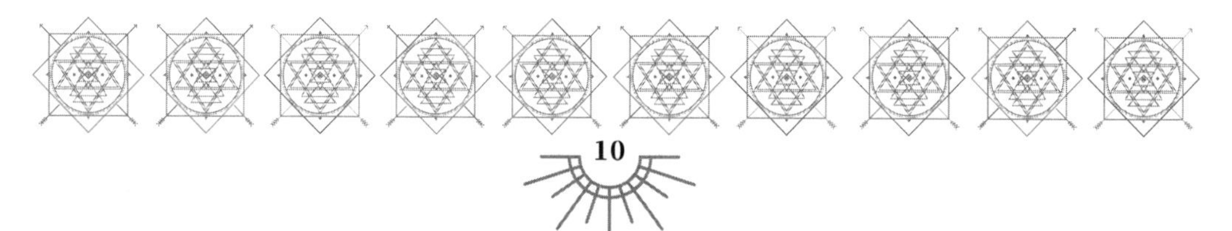

uses eggs rolled on the ground, spun or passed from the hands of those who have questions to the hands of those with answers.

PALMISTRY

In this ancient art, the lines, mounds, and shape of the hands, fingers, and nails form the basis for assessments of the character and the future of those having their palms read. The mounds (or mounts) are linked with the planets, marrying palmistry and astrology (see above).

PEGOMANCY

Spring water, and the way it bubbles up through natural fountains, is analyzed by pegomancers.

PHYSCHOGRAPHY

Physchographers are in tune with a spiritual force that "tells" those blessed with the gift what to write—sometimes, but not always, when the seer is in a trance.

PHYSIOGNOMY

Practitioners of this art study the physical features of a person's face to assess their character and their future.

PYROMANCY

Also known as pyroscopy, pyromancy is a general term for divining the future by studying fire and flame.

RADIESTHESIA

This is a general term for divination that uses a device such as a divining rod or pendulum.

RHAPSODOMANCY

Those with the gift of rhapsodamancy use a book of poetry opened at random and a chance-chosen passage on the page. The practice is a branch of stichomancy (see below) and bibliomancy (see above).

SCIOMANCY

Sciomancers are mediums by another name—people with the gift of communicating with spirit guides, usually when in a trance-like state.

SCRYING

Scrying is divination via a range of methods, from smoke to shells.

SORTILEGE

Those who practice sortilege draw lots and interpret the shapes they make when they fall.

SPODOMANCY

Spodomancy involves deciphering the patterns seen in cinders and soot.

STICHOMANCY

Like rhapsodomancy, stichomancy uses the printed word to foretell events. But whereas the latter relies on poetry, stichomancy can be done with any book (see also bibliomancy).

TASSEOGRAPHY

After loose-leaf tea has been drunk, the cup is placed upside down on a saucer to drain it completely, and the shapes formed by the leaves remaining inside the cup are interpreted.

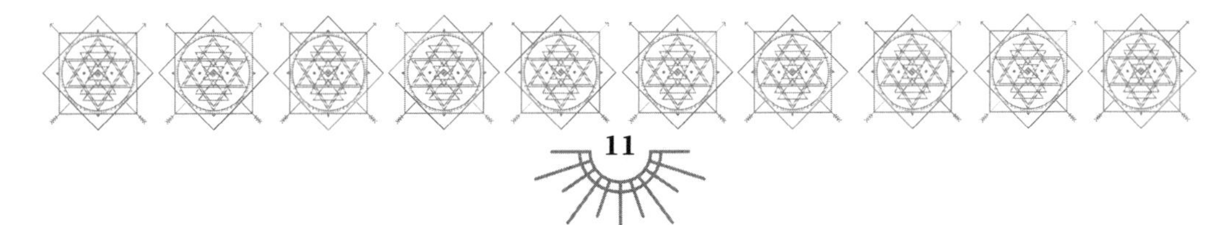

1

Tea-leaf reading

Reading tea leaves—tasseography—has a long and noble history that began in China, perhaps as early as 3000 BCE. According to legend, the first tea came about by accident when the leaves fell into a pot of water.

True or not, what we do know is that tea-drinking spread throughout the Far East and India, from whence it, and the associated divination, came to Europe.

Tea was a luxury in Britain (so expensive it was kept under lock and key) until the nineteenth century, when large quantities were imported from India and Ceylon (present-day Sri Lanka). So tasseography was a rare skill. But the art of divination from the dregs was practiced long before that. The Ancient Greeks probably studied the dregs in wine glasses for clues to what the future held, and whenever herbal remedies were brewed to give to the sick, what remained in the cup would be peered at by a spey wife (a Scottish expression for a woman who has divinatory skills).

Everyone who reads tea leaves has their own rituals and interpretations. Some pour the tea into a cup through a strainer and either use what is there to peer into the future, or do so in association with the leaves left in the cup after it has been drunk.

It is good to use traditional tea, the leaves of which are separate and firm, such as Earl Grey or Darjeeling. Make the tea as you usually would: most people swirl boiling water around in the pot to warm it before adding the leaves; one spoonful per person and "one for the pot" is the standard recipe.

As the tea is brewing (three to four minutes is usually enough), ask whoever has questions they need an answer for to concentrate on them. It's not cheating to ask them what it is that concerns them. Pour the tea into plain white cups and enjoy drinking it—don't rush, just sip it as usual. If you want to continue concentrating, that's fine. If you want to enjoy a chat (a euphemism for a good gossip),

that's all right too, for one of the secrets of successful tea-leaf reading is relaxation.

When the moment comes, it's time to get down to business. As mentioned, rituals vary. One trusted method is for the querent to take the cup in their left hand and swirl it three times widdershins (counterclockwise) for a woman, and clockwise for a man. The cup is then placed rim down on the saucer to drain away any remaining tea. The reader should then take the cup in their own left hand and interpret the patterns the leaves have made. As with all other methods of divination, let instinct be your guide.

It's not just the leaves that are important—the place inside the cup where the shapes form also influences things. For convenience, it helps to think of the cup as divided into four quarters.

The quarter nearest the handle represents the querent. Leaves that stick to the cup in this area are concerned with him or her, their home, and those closest to them. Depending on the images, clumps of leaves that stick to the cup here could suggest that the questioner is being overwhelmed by responsibility for family and close friends, or it can mean that their home and personal life is particularly rich.

The side opposite the handle is concerned with strangers, acquaintances (rather than friends), the workplace, travel and other matters away from home. A large concentration here suggests that these matters concern the querent more than the family and the home.

To the left of the handle (from the seer's angle) is the area that stands for the past, with people moving out of the querent's ken. Unusually large areas here indicate that things unresolved in the past are having a bearing on the questioner's life. This is reinforced if there is an especially large concentration of leaves in this area, and if they are particularly dark.

The part of the cup to the reader's right is the area where leaves represent upcoming events and people who are about to have an influence on the querent's life. If there are no leaves here, it should not be taken as a bad omen, or that there is no future. Rather, that the questioner is more concerned with the present and the past than with what life holds in store.

As well as being divided into four quarters, the cup is also divided (metaphorically speaking) horizontally. Images close to the rim indicate the present—days and weeks—while those clinging to the lower part indicate the more distant future—months and years.

According to Romany tradition, a dry cup heralds good news. But if there is a trace of liquid remaining in the cup, there will be tears before the week is out. They also believe the rim of the cup equates with joy and happiness, the bottom with sorrow.

An A–Z of shapes

Different symbols often mean different things to different readers. To one well-known tasseographer, an acorn indicates a pregnancy, with a nearby initial giving a clue as to who will be so blessed. To another, the same symbol near the rim of the cup foretells financial success; in the middle it is equated with good health; and at the bottom it is an indication that both health and finances are due for a boost. A third reader sees it as a sign of health and plenty.

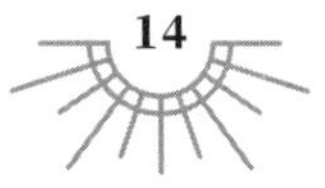

What follows is a general guide to some of the most commonly seen symbols.

Airplanes presage an unexpected journey that might be linked with a disappointment. It may also mean new projects and a rise in status.

Anchors mean a journey will come to a successful end, and if the querent is having difficulties, stability will soon be restored. At the top of the cup, an anchor can indicate a boost in business; in the middle, a voyage that boosts prosperity is indicated; and if it's near the bottom, social success is beckoning.

Angels herald good news.

Ants suggest industry and hard work, perhaps working with others to bring a project to a happy completion.

Arches link the querent with marriage or long-term relationships. Someone regarded as an enemy may be about to extend the hand of friendship.

Arrows usually mean bad news. If the arrow is pointing toward the querent, he or she may be in danger of an attack; pointing away, they may find themselves on the offensive. Others see arrows as the bearers of good news in career and financial matters.

Axes may mean the questioner has to chop away unpleasant difficulties.

Babies presage new interests.

Baggage—the kind you travel with—can mean the obvious. It can also signify that the questioner is holding on to unnecessary emotional baggage that should be dumped.

Bags are a warning that a trap may be about to ensnare the querent.

Balls say that the querent will bounce back from difficulties. Balls can also suggest that someone involved in sports will have a significant influence, probably bringing a changeable future.

Balls and chains are a sign that current commitments may be hard to shed, but that they should be.

Balloons suggest that troubles may float in, but they will soon drift off again.

Bears suggest travel to a foreign country. A bear can also say that a strong ally will offer protection in a time of need; he or she will give you strength to resolve a difficult situation.

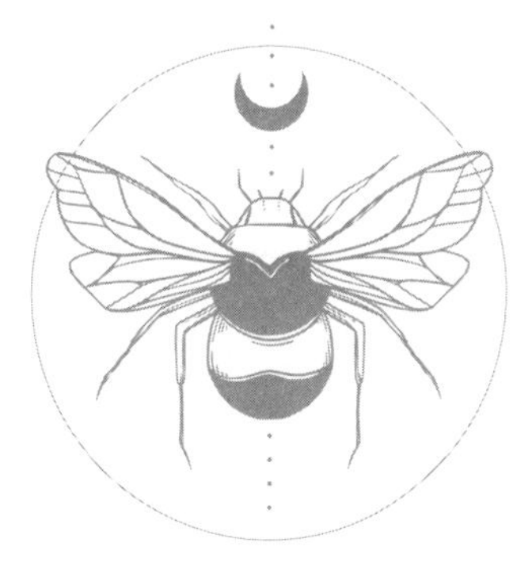

Bees bring news that change is in store for family or close friends.

Bells chime that marriage is in the air.

Birds bring good news. If they are flying away from the handle, a departure could be around the corner; perhaps a fledgling is about to leave the nest. If they are winging their way toward the handle, a new opportunity is on the way.

Boats are an indication that an important discovery is on the horizon. A boat also signifies a visit from a friend, and signals that soon a safe harbor will be reached.

Books, if open, suggest that startling revelations are coming. An open book also says that to move ahead, a secret may need to be shared. It is also a sign that legal action could follow, but that if that happens, there will be a successful outcome. A closed book means that a delay will affect plans.

Boots may be a sign that caution is needed. Others say a boot means achievement, and that if the querent is seeking protection, it will be theirs. But if the boot is pointing away from the handle, a dismissal is coming. And if they are broken, a failure looms.

Bottles may foretell illness, but one on its own says that the querent's life will soon be bubbling over with pleasure. A full bottle is an encouraging sign to channel energy into a new challenge. An empty one is a sign of exhaustion, and that health may soon be a cause for concern. A half-full one? It could be half-empty! And that's the difference between an optimist and a pessimist.

Branches, if in leaf, herald a birth. If bare, disappointment looms.

Bridges present an opportunity for success that will soon cross the querent's path.

Brooms sweep change into life, suggesting that a good clearout (physical or emotional) might be a good thing.

Buildings suggest a change of address.

Butterflies say that innocent pleasures are about to flutter through the questioner's life, offering regeneration, and encouraging a carefree attitude pays dividends.

Cannons see **Guns**.

Castles denote that circumstances are about to improve, especially if the questioner harbors a desire for luxury and pampering. They can also say that outside events affecting people who are not members of the immediate family are interfering with domestic happiness.

Cats indicate treachery, something that is reinforced if the feline's back is arched.

Chains are a sign that links with other people will strengthen the sense of purpose.

Cherries mean that a victory is imminent.

Chessmen say that a short-term project should be put to one side, and that it is time to plan for the long term if looming troubles are to be overcome. They also indicate that people are maneuvering into position for a conflict, and that it is time for the querent to follow their example.

Cliffs warn that the querent may be about to walk into a dangerous situation. But they can also suggest that the time has come to cast convention aside and live a little dangerously.

Clouds darken the bright skies of life with doubt, but they should clear—eventually.

Clover is regarded as a lucky symbol in reality, and it retains those connotations in the teacup, heralding prosperity.

Coffins signify if not death, then a loss.

Coins are a sign that money is coming.

Cows foretell prosperity and tranquil times. Enjoy them while they last—the herd may soon move on to greener pastures.

Crowns say that an honor or legacy is about to grace the questioner, along with the chance of a dream coming true.

Daffodils are a welcome harbinger not just of spring, but of imminent wealth.

Dice are a sign that now is the time to take a risk and wait for the good times to roll in.

Dogs, famed for their friendship and loyalty, say that good friends are coming the querent's way, especially if they seem to be running toward the handle.

Donkeys are a sign that says, "Be patient and things will work out."

Doors offer a potentially exciting step into the unknown that can be taken with confidence if the door is open, but not if the door is closed, as the area on the other side of the door is not yet ready to be trodden upon.

Dots, as well as speaking of money-making opportunities, emphasize the meaning of any nearby symbol.

Ducks speak of travel by water, and of opportunity swimming in from abroad. Ducks may also say that if the querent has been searching for his natural role in life, the search may soon be over.

Drums tell of quarrels and disagreements, scandal and gossip; to see them in the teacup is a call to action.

Ears are a sign that the questioner should be on the alert because malicious rumors are being spread about them. They should be on the lookout for false friends.

Eggs signify an increase, perhaps springing from a new project.

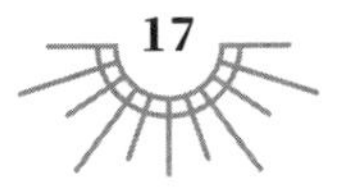

Elephants signify wisdom and a success, maybe thanks to the efforts of a trustworthy friend.

Eyes are a warning to act carefully in the coming weeks.

Faces, when smiling, are a sign of happiness. When frowning, they say that opposition will soon stand in the way of progress.

Fans herald flirtation, maybe leading to an indiscretion.

Feathers are a sign that indiscretion and instability will upset the questioner—but not too seriously.

Feet suggest that an important decision will have to be made in the near future, and if it is to lead to success, the querent will have to act quickly. Feet also say that the querent may have to look way beyond his own backyard to find it.

Fences warn that restrictions are about to be imposed on the querent's options, perhaps because someone is being overprotective.

Fingers—when pointing to another sign—emphasize the second sign's meaning.

Fish tell of good fortune, often the result of lucky speculation. They can also indicate that foreign travel is on the horizon.

Flags bring a warning of danger and suggest that to overcome it, the querent will need to rally resources and act courageously.

Flies indicate irritating little things that will annoy the querent for a while.

Flowers presage a celebration. **Flowers** also signify that the questioner will be showered with small kindnesses that will make life worth living. One bloom can mean that love is about to appear; several say that if the questioner is about to face an interview, there is nothing to worry about. Flowers in form of a garland herald a promotion.

Forks are a warning to beware flattery and false friends.

Fountains indicate that success lies in store. They also mean that he or she is more interested in sexual passion than romantic love.

Foxes signify sagacity and foresight. They tell the querent that if she cannot achieve her aims by using persuasion, there is nothing wrong with subtlety or even stealth—but not at the expense of honesty.

Frogs are an indication that the questioner is good at fitting in. Frogs can also presage change—perhaps a change of address.

Fruit is a sign of prosperous times.

Gallows warn that a loss is imminent. It might be financial, or it could indicate the loss of a good friend. They can also suggest that the querent is feeling locked into a potentially dangerous situation from which they see no means of escape, but desperately want to find one. Conversely, if the questioner is not in the best of health, gallows are a sign of an upturn.

Gates, when open, presage prosperity and happiness. But when closed, they should be taken as a warning to be on guard against a loss, perhaps financial or material.

Guitars presage harmony, perhaps leading to romance. They can also indicate a vain nature and a tendency to be irritable with those whom the querent considers to be of inferior talent.

Guns say that if other people's inertia has been impeding progress, now is the time to cut ties. Guns are also a warning that unless properly channeled, an outburst of aggression may have unfortunate results.

Hammocks suspended between two trees suggest an unconventional nature, and perhaps a desire to shirk responsibilities and take it easy.

Hands, when open, say that a new friendship is coming and that it will be mutually beneficial. If closed, someone is about to act in a mean way, which is quite out of character.

Hats signal that change is the air, maybe in the form of a new job. They can also herald the arrival of an unexpected visitor (perhaps an old rival) or an invitation to a formal occasion.

Heads alert the querent to be on the lookout for new opportunities that could result in a promotion to a new position of authority.

Hearts whisper that a new friendship is around the corner, or has already presented itself. It could lead to romance or marriage. Hearts also indicate that a family situation is developing that should be handled with tremendous tact and sensitivity if it is not to end in a rift.

Hens cluck that an older person, probably a motherly type, will have an increasing influence in the querent's life, but that her fussiness will become more and more irritating.

Hills should be taken as a warning that the path ahead may become blocked. The problems will be little, and easily overcome, and when they are, long-term ambitions will be achieved.

Horns are a welcome sign—cornucopias that will bring with them an abundance of happiness and peace.

Horses bring news of a lover, especially if just the head is seen. They also indicate general good news. If they are at full gallop across the cup, it may be time to get traveling. If they are harnessed to a cart, they signify that a change of job or address is beckoning—a very advantageous one if the cart is full.

Horseshoes herald good fortune.

Houses can indicate that there is nothing to fear in the immediately future, for they bring security. They can also say that domestic matters are about to take up an increasing amount of time.

Icebergs are a sign that someone the querent knows has hidden depths, and that if they are not recognized, there could be trouble in store.

Initials represent the people for whom they stand, and say that nearby signs refer to them rather than to the querent.

Ink spilled in the cup represents doubts that must be clarified before the querent signs an important document, possibly a legal one.

Insects suggest little problems will irritate the querent. Nothing serious—just thoroughly annoying, like a buzzing housefly that you keep swatting but never manage to get.

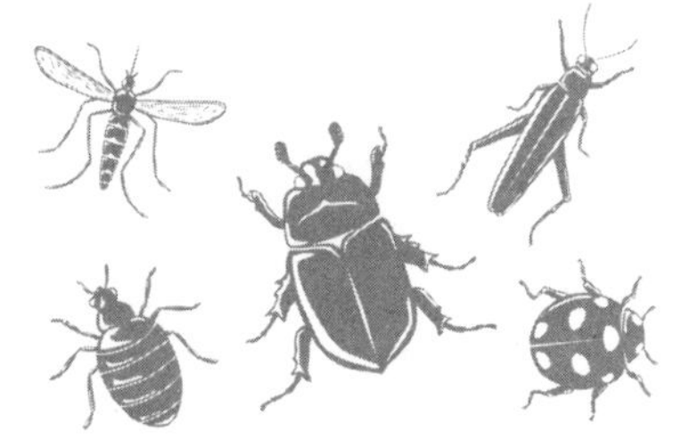

Jewels say that someone is about to bestow an unexpected gift of a generous nature on the querent.

Kettles tell of domestic happiness—as long as they are near the handle. But if they are near the bottom of the cup, the opposite holds true.

Keys are a sign of enlightenment and of new opportunities, unless there are two of them at the bottom of the cup. If so, lock the doors and fasten the windows, for they warn of a burglary. They also signify an increasingly independent nature, perhaps of a child about to flee the nest.

Kings can warn that an older person may act in a high-handed manner that could be upsetting. But it could be that he or she is acting out of a genuine desire to help, and should be regarded as a powerful ally.

Kites, soaring around the cup, speak of lofty aspirations being successfully achieved.

Knives warn that a relationship is about to come to an end—the closer they are to the top of the cup, the closer that relationship will be. If at the very top, divorce is in the air. At the bottom, lawsuits beckon—the closer to the bottom, the more acrimony will they bring. Anywhere else, they say, "Beware of false friends!"

Ladders suggest that an advancement will present itself to the querent— a promotion at work, or something more spiritual. They are also a sign that it's time to set sights high.

Leaves are a sign of good fortune and prosperity. Falling leaves hint that, come autumn, a natural turning point will be reached that will bring a surge of happiness.

Lines have different meanings, depending on whether they are straight, slanting or curvy. Straight ones suggest progress, perhaps through a journey. Slanting lines speak of failure in business. And curved, wavy ones herald disappointments and uncertainty lying in wait.

Lions—the kings of the jungle—signify powerful friends.

Lizards are a sign to get in touch with primitive instincts, and to trust them. They are also a warning to check facts extremely carefully, as the source may not be as reliable as it seems.

Loops indicate that the path ahead is a crooked one; the end is in sight, but it's taking forever, as pointless disagreements and unwise decisions make the journey seem interminable.

Magnets mean that a new interest will become increasingly important—and it could well be a romantic interest, someone who is magnetically attractive and absolutely irresistible.

Men mean visitors; if their arms are outstretched, they are bearing gifts, so welcome them.

Mermaids sing that passion will lead to temptation, temptation to infidelity and infidelity to heartbreak.

Mice may foretell of poverty, perhaps as the result of theft. They also say that this is not the time to be timid, and that if initiative is taken, benefits will be substantial.

Mirrors might indicate that the querent is vain by nature, or that they feel life is passing them by.

Moles (animals) suggest that secrets are in the air and that, when revealed, they will have a significant effect on the questioner's life. They may also mean that a false friend is doing something that will undermine the querent in some way.

The Moon is a frequently seen symbol. If it is a full moon, a love affair is in the works. If it is a waxing moon, new projects will prosper. If it's waning, a decline in fortune is indicated. If it is partially obscured, depression is about to cloud the querent's life. And if it is surrounded by tiny fragments of tea leaves, marriage is in the air—but for money, rather than love.

Mountains can be a sign that serious obstacles will appear, blocking the querent's view of the future. But they also stand for high ambitions that may or may not be achieved, depending on what else is in the cup.

Nails suggest that the querent is about to experience malice, pain, and injustice. To get what is due, the querent will have to fight hard.

Necklaces suggest a secret admirer who, when they present themselves, may turn out to be "the one." A broken necklace, though, warns of a friendship that may be about to cool.

Needles have a trilogy of meanings. They can say that a quarrel is about to be settled to everyone's satisfaction. They might suggest that the best way to deal with jealous criticism is to brush it to one side. And, finally, they could say that an unsatisfactory situation is being tolerated in the hope that something will happen to make things better.

Nests say that domestic matters are about to come to the fore, and that someone is about

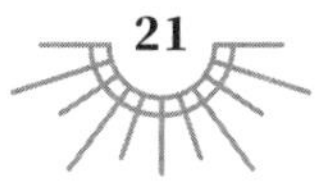

to ask for the key to the door and become a visitor rather than a resident.

Nets can be taken as a sign that the questioner may be feeling trapped or worried about a new venture. They can mean that something that has long been looked for is about to appear.

Numbers, close to a leaf or leaves that indicate an upcoming event in the querent's life, tell the number of days that will elapse before that event will occur. Some numbers, though, have their own meanings. One signposts creativity, energy, and new beginnings. Two is a sign of duality and rivalry, while three sometimes promises a betrothal. Four says that it's time to accept that resources are limited, and to work within them. Five is a sign that clear communication is needed when dealing with others. Six heralds peaceful and harmonious times. Seven points toward the unconscious world, and says that it is time to put things into long-term perspective. Eight cautions the querent to follow convention, while nine suggests self-interest, as well as being a sign of a project completed satisfactorily.

Oars say that the time has come to stop waiting for others to help, and to find a solution to whatever ails, perhaps by moving to a new house or new job.

Octopuses suggest that danger is about to entwine the querent in its tentacles, probably because he or she has overstretched available resources and taken on too much, either in business or in their personal life. On a happier note, they can also represent a multi-talented person who will be happy to oblige.

Ostriches, said to bury their heads in the sand when danger threatens, indicate that the questioner shares that trait.

Owls warn that there's trouble afoot. The trouble in question could be brought about by gossip and scandal, or perhaps a failure. They also warn of neglected tasks. But they have a good meaning, too, signifying that a wise person is standing by to help.

Padlocks, when they are open, offer the promise of getting out of a difficult situation or unwanted arrangement. When they are closed, unspoken concerns about a job or a domestic matter are starting to bring their weight to bear.

Palm trees say that success will bring honor to the questioner, who may be feeling a need to be cherished by family and friends. They may also be a sign that travel is on the horizon.

Parachutes announce that help is at hand if the querent is feeling vulnerable. They can also mean that fear of failure or impending disaster can be dismissed; it is completely unfounded.

Peacocks promise that the querent's desire for a more luxurious lifestyle may soon be fulfilled. But they can also say that the vanity of friends poses a threat.

Pendulums signify that the questioner needs to put some effort into restoring harmony with family, friends, and colleagues. Another meaning is that there is a change of course on the cards, and a third is a warning not to take things at face value, to look below the surface to establish the reality of a situation.

Pigs might represent a generous, extremely hospitable friend, or they can warn that over-indulgence could lead to ill health.

Pigeons may suggest that an unexpected communication will be received from a far-off place, and that the bearer of the news is someone in whom the querent can have absolute confidence.

Pipes suggest that if thought is given to a problem, the solution will appear.

Pistols warn of danger and indicate that someone will use unpleasant methods to get their way at the expense of the questioner.

Purses presage luck or gain, depending on whether they are open or closed. They tend to turn up in the cups of people who have deep pockets and short arms.

Pyramids indicate a concern with healing and psychic powers. If they appear in the leaves of someone who has a pressing problem, the answer to it lies in the past, not in the present.

Question marks suggest that caution should be used in the coming days.

Rabbits say that speed is of the essence, especially if there are enemies to confront. They can also indicate that the querent is concerned with fertility.

Rainbows signify that, while some wishes may be fulfilled soon, more unrealistic ones may have to be put on hold.

Rats warn the querent to be on the lookout for a vindictive, deceitful person who has revenge in mind. On a brighter note, they might be saying that if open-handed methods have failed the querent, then now might be the time to try underhanded ones!

Rings, if they are close to the top, mean that marriage is around the corner. If in the middle, a proposal can be expected in the near, but not immediate, future. If at the bottom, the engagement will be a long one. The marriage will be a happy one if the ring is complete. If it is broken, the engagement will be called off before the couple walks down the aisle.

Roads suggest that a new path is about to appear in the questioner's life. If they are straight, fine. But a fork suggests that a choice will have to be made—the wider the fork, the more important the choice.

Scales are a sign of justice and judgment. The judgment could be significant. Balanced scales suggest that a just, fair decision will bring benefits; unbalanced ones that the questioner will suffer injustice.

Scissors presage domestic arguments that will become so bitter that separation is on the cards.

Seesaws can mean that mood swings will make the querent lightheaded with happiness one minute, down in the dumps the next. They can also indicate that the ups and downs of life will make it hard to achieve a sense of balance.

Sharks say that force may be required if attacks from an unexpected source are to be repelled with any chance of success.

Shells mean that good news is coming in with the tide. They also indicate intuitive wisdom and tell the questioner to listen to the inner voice, or instinct, and act on it.

Ships can say that an increase is on the horizon. They can also suggest that if the querent is worried about something, they can cast any doubts overboard, because it will come to a successful conclusion.

Snakes suggest that it is time for the querent to—metaphorically speaking—get rid of current burdens and responsibilities, and move, regenerated, toward the future.

Spiders may suggest that someone is spinning a web of subterfuge that will soon enmesh the questioner. To others, it says that persistence will pay off financially.

Spinning wheels say two things: that careful planning and consistent industry will bring good results, or that someone is plotting behind the scenes to the querent's detriment.

Squares were once seen as signs of restriction, but now they're taken to mean that protection is there for the asking. They also say that if the querent uses the near future to make careful long-term plans, it will lead to a boost of financial and material prospects.

Squirrels carry the message that people who save for the future have less to worry about than those who live for today.

Stars bring messages of hope, particularly where health matters are concerned. If it has five points, good fortune is there for the asking. If it has eight points, accidents will cause reversals. If there are five stars in the cup, success will come, but it will not bring happiness. And seven stars say that grief may be imminent.

The Sun says that the gray skies of disappointment will soon clear, and happiness will beam down on the querent, bringing success and perhaps power. It may also mean that next summer will be an especially happy one, perhaps involving travel to a sunny destination.

Swords suggest that the querent should prepare for quarrels and disputes.

Tables indicate that social life is about to take a lively and positive upturn.

Teapots presage meetings—long, boring ones that will make the querent come to the conclusion that any meeting of more than two people is a waste of time.

Telescopes say that the answers to mysteries will soon be revealed, but that these answers lie outside the immediate environment.

Tents indicate a love of adventure, but one that could lead to an unsettled life.

Tortoises and turtles say that while success can be achieved, it will be a long time coming. They also indicate a love of tradition.

Towers can imply that the querent is feeling restricted, unless they have steps, in which case they lead to a rise in status and a financial boost. A tower that is incomplete suggests that plans are not finished—and never will be.

Trees augur prosperity brought about by long-held ambitions coming to happy fruition. Romany folk believe that if the tree is surrounded by smaller leaves, then the ambitions will be realized in the country, or at least they will be associated with it.

Triangles can mean unexpected success or unexpected failure. Upward is good, and downward is bad, unless the querent realizes there's still time to grab an opportunity that's about to slip from their hands.

Tunnels promise that confusion and setbacks will soon be swept away, but only if the querent probes in the right places.

Umbrellas suggest that little annoyances are about to shower the questioner. They also signify a need for shelter. If they are open, shelter will be found; if closed, it will not be.

Unicorns offer the promise of magical insights that illumine the querent's life in some way. They also promise that unusual and unexpected opportunity is on the horizon.

Vans bring movement in their wake.

Violins see **Guitars**.

Volcanoes presage that an eruption of passion will sweep the querent off their feet. They often appear when the person whose leaves are being read is seething with anger, but is determined not to let it show.

Walking sticks herald the arrival of a visitor.

Waterfalls bring prosperity.

Weather vanes point to inconsistent and indecisive friends. They warn the querent to be on the lookout for signs of change that, if recognized and acted on when the time is right, will lead to some benefit.

Webs, like spiders, are a sign that deceit and subterfuge will have a significant bearing on the querent's life.

Whales promise the fulfillment of a big undertaking. They offer commercial and professional success if the querent is involved in one of the caring professions.

Wheels, if they are complete, say that good fortune is about to roll in. If they are near the rim of the cup, then good fortune will come in the form of an unexpected legacy or win. If it's broken, disappointments loom.

Windows can mean good luck or bad luck, depending on whether they are open or shut. They may offer new insights or a chance to explore new horizons, unless they are curtained, in which case they point to the fact that other people's narrow horizons are holding the querent back.

2

Crystal divination

Think of divination and one of the stereotypical images that probably comes to mind is that of an old woman peering into a crystal ball and making relevant what she sees in it to whichever question has been put to her.

This image of the crystal gazer has probably done more to harm divination's reputation than any other, which is sad, because crystal gazing has a long and honorable tradition as part of scrying—using crystals, mirrors, flames, and water as a means to peer into the future.

Traditionally, the ball used for crystal gazing was a gift from someone with the talent; nowadays they are available in a variety of crystals—clear or smoky quartz, beryl and obsidian are the most popular—and glass. Glass ones should be examined closely for blemishes or bubbles, as they could be distracting.

When buying one, the mood should be relaxed and receptive, an atmosphere encouraged in spiritual shops, not just by the incense that is often burned there but also by the positive vibrations of the staff. Handle several crystal balls, which are usually about four inches (ten centimeters) in diameter. How do they fit in the hands? Are they perfectly plain spheres, or do they have angles and planes inside them? Most people find that when they go to buy a crystal ball, they keep returning to one, no matter how many they look at and handle. If this happens, that is the ball to buy.

To prepare the ball, wash it in a mild solution of vinegar and water, then polish it with a soft cloth. When it is not being used, the ball should be wrapped in a cloth and kept out of direct sunlight, which affects sensitivity. It should not be handled by anyone other than the user. Some gazers unwrap their crystal ball and put it in a moonlit place during a full moon, which they believe enhances the crystal's power.

Crystals pick up vibrations when handled by other people. If someone is to handle another person's crystal ball,

the hands must be cupped around it and, after use, the ball should be washed in vinegar or water, or held under running water while visualizing it surrounded with bright, shining light. Then it should be wrapped in silk or velvet until it is used again.

How they work

When gazing into a crystal ball, intuition should be focused, the rational mind suspended. Soft, gentle light reflects off the crystal, catching the eye and holding it firm.

Soon, the eyes go slightly out of focus and the ball mists over; inside the mist, images start to form. These images are projections from the gazer's subconscious mind or inner crystal.

The room should be a quiet place where the gazer will not be disturbed, and lit, in the words of one gazer, "like daylight on a wet, cloudy day." Some people use candlelight to achieve this, others drape lamps in a suitable (flame-retardant) cloth.

It is essential that the gazer is in a relaxed state of mind before beginning. Some people can achieve this with deep breathing, while others use visualization. As this is being achieved, the crystal should be held in the hands for a few moments to attune the ball to the gazer's vibrations. At the same time, questions can be framed, and safe solutions considered, but not pondered too deeply.

The ball is now placed on a black silk or velvet cloth, and perhaps partially surrounded with a black velvet or silk curtain or screen. Now stare at the crystal until the eyes go out of focus, the mist forms and images appear inside it. These images must not be forced; they should arise naturally. The images may appear in the ball or in the mind's eye. Even meaningless ones might have significance, so write everything down as it arises.

It takes time and concentration to gaze successfully into a crystal. But not too much time, and learning to concentrate is a talent that has many other applications, so it is well worth the effort. The first occasion should last no longer than ten minutes; gradually increase the time of each session, at first to fifteen minutes, then twenty, and so on. But sessions should never last longer than an hour. Time each session with a watch or clock positioned so that you can see its face but will not be distracted by it.

The presence of another person distracts concentration at first. With experience comes the ability to answer the questions of others, as long as they are asked in a hushed voice.

Gazers often find that small, glittering points of light appear in the mist before it clears, and what has been described as an ocean of blue space appears, inside of which visions appear. These visions are sometimes symbolic; the meanings of these symbols are similar to those seen in a tea-leaf reading (see pages 12-25)—or they may be scenic. Visions that appear in the background lie further ahead than those that are in the foreground, which denote either the present or the immediate future.

When images come, no effort should be made to keep them there; they should be allowed to ebb and flow, like the tide.

CRYSTAL CLEAR

Crystal-ball reading is not the only use for crystals. A variety of small crystals, kept in a

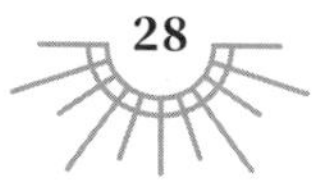

special bag, can also be used. The simplest way is to shake the bag and, while focusing on a question, take out the first two or three that the fingers touch. As they are drawn, take a moment to see if the answer comes spontaneously to mind, before looking up the meaning of the crystals.

Boards for throwing crystals are available from specialist shops; the combination of the answers on the board and the sagacity of the crystals have satisfied countless users.

Generally, red, yellow, orange, and sparkling-white (hot-colored) stones contain a great deal of creative energy and mean that some action is indicated with regard to the area with which the stone is associated. Green, blue, purple, pink, and pearly white stones reflect spiritual desires, thoughts, and emotions.

The associations of some common crystals are shown below.

- **AGATE**
  Success in worldly matters
- **AMETHYST**
  Shifts in consciousness and life changes
- **BLACK AGATE**
  Prosperity and courage
- **BLUE LACE AGATE**
  A need for healing
- **RED AGATE**
  Longevity and good health
- **AVENTURINE**
  Growth and expansion
- **CITRINE**
  Wisdom in celestial matters
- **DIAMOND**
  Permanence
- **EMERALD**
  Fertility
- **JADE**
  Immortality and perfection
- **RED JASPER**
  Worldly affairs
- **LAPIS LAZULI**
  Favored by the divine
- **CLEAR QUARTZ**
  Self-healing and love
- **SAPPHIRE**
  Chastity and truth
- **SNOWFLAKE OBSIDIAN**
  Closure of a challenging time
- **TIGER' S EYE**
  The need to look beneath the surface
- **WHITE QUARTZ**
  Change of a profound nature
- **UNAKITE**
  Integration and composure

3

Chinese astrology

Divination has been practiced in Asia and India for thousands of years. Whereas Westerners pay little attention to divination (although even the most cynical among them still consult their daily horoscope), to millions of Chinese, astrology and the I Ching are part of everyday life.

Whereas in Western astrology the Sun is central, Chinese astrologers look to the Moon for their inspiration. It is also influenced by, among other things, the five elements: Earth, Metal, Wood, Water, and Fire. For example, a Fire Pig will have different characteristics from an Earth Pig, and a Water Rat will differ from a Metal Rat. Those seeking deeper knowledge should consult the Internet or bookshops that specialize on the subject.

Each sign shows the main years attributed to it. But remember, the lunar year does not run from January to December. You will see that in several years, one of the "months" is almost twice the length of the others. This is because, although there are usually twelve lunar months each year, in leap years there are thirteen. The names are seasonal in nature and, because the thirteenth month can occur in any season, the leap year Moon is wedded to the Moon that precedes it, and those born on any date in the two-month period will share characteristics.

Thousands of years ago, the lives of the people who lived in the Yellow River Valley were subject to floods and hailstorms, searing heat and devastating droughts—all of which were blamed on the movements of the stars and the planets. Documents dating from the period correlate natural events to heavenly happenings. A flood may occur during an eclipse of the Moon; a drought may have hit when one of the planets was seen in a particular place in the night sky. Over the centuries, a vast body of

knowledge about the cyclical nature of the universe was perceived.

Between 1500 and 1100 BCE, the sages who recorded and pondered these events were thought to have divinatory powers, and they were promoted to positions of political power and influence. Being aware of the psychology of ordinary people, these wise and ambitious men evolved a system that was eventually codified by philosophers who, to use a modern expression, put their own spin on things. They believed that if the known universe was influenced by recognizable cycles, then so was the nature of man. In a perfect world, the philosophers decreed, everyone would live for sixty years, which were divided by the five elements— Earth, Metal, Wood, Water, and Fire—resulting in twelve earthly branches, which would evolve into twelve years, each of which was assigned an animal. Each animal sign was then divided into lunar months, each of which, in turn, was ascribed certain attributes.

In Chinese astrology, the celestial bodies recorded in the second millennium bce still follow the same paths through the heavens, continuing to influence us.

As with many things Chinese—philosophy, medicine, and astrology, to name just a few—the concept that underlies ancient and modern thought and practice is Yin and Yang. They combine to make up the life force, Qi. In his famous book *Canon of Internal Medicine*, the Yellow Emperor claims that Yin and Yang constitute the basic principle that governs the entire universe, so it is not surprising that the years and months of the Chinese calendar have Yin and Yang aspects.

Yin is soft, dark, cold, and wet; its symbol is a cloud-topped mountain. Yang is hard, bright, hot, and dry; its symbol is a sun at the center of a crown of shining rays. In medicine, perfect health depends on achieving a balance between the two, as does perfect peace of mind. In Chinese astrology, a Yin year can modify a Yang month and a Yang month a Yin year, something that has to be taken into account when using Chinese astrology to divine the future. Chinese astrology is based on years consisting of twelve months running in cycles of twelve years. Each twelve-month period is named after an animal that rules for a year. In the beginning, these cycles were referred to as the Twelve Branches, but over time they were given the characteristics of twelve animals.

Why these twelve animals? One legend has it that Buddha invited all the beasts in the kingdom to celebrate the New Year with him, but only twelve arrived. The Buddha rewarded them by naming a year in their honor. The Rat, the first to arrive, was accorded the honor of having the first year in the cycle named after him. The last year was named after the last animal to arrive: the Pig. But there is no mention of these animals in the texts of the Han Dynasty. A more likely explanation is offered by those who believe the names were taken to China from Central Asia, perhaps as recently as 800 CE.

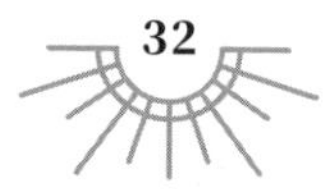

The 12 Signs

The twelve signs are the Rat, the Ox, the Tiger, the Rabbit, the Dragon, the Snake, the Horse, the Ram, the Monkey, the Rooster, the Dog, and the Pig. The Dragon is the only mythological beast in the menagerie and, although it is a frightening beast to Westerners, it is seen as something of a benefactor to the Chinese. Each of the animals has well-defined characteristics, and those born in the year of a certain animal are thought to possess its qualities.

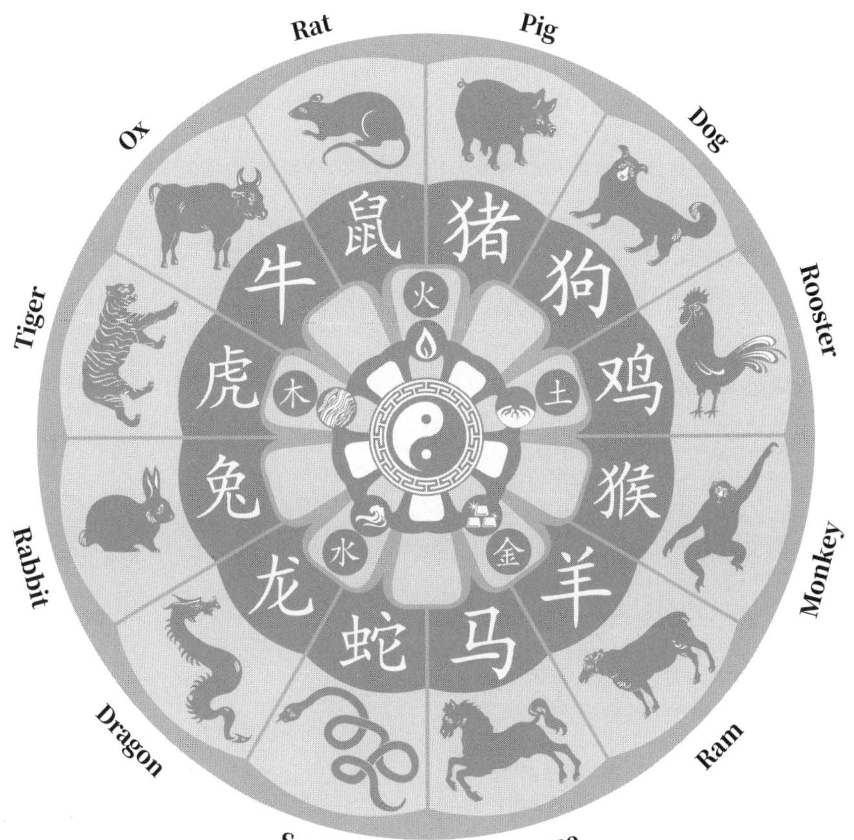

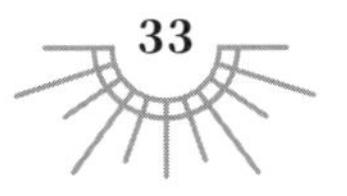

The Chinese New Year starts on the first day of the first Moon (see below), usually at the end of January or beginning of February. And whereas the Western calendar adds an extra day to every fourth February to balance the monthly lunar cycle with the solar year, the Chinese add an extra month every seven years over a nineteen-year cycle. Therefore it is not possible to ascribe an exact Western year to each of the signs in the Chinese horoscope. Someone born in 1995 would be a Dog if he was born between January 1st and 30th, but a Pig if he was born after that date.

Each year is also ascribed one of the five elements: Earth, Metal, Wood, Water, and Fire. And each element straddles two years in succession before ceding power to the next in line. So, whereas all Monkeys share common attributes, they are not necessarily influenced by the same element; a Metal Monkey will have different characteristics from a Water Monkey.

Metal people tend to be rigid. So, while all Oxen can be stubborn, a Metal Ox will be even more so. Metal people insist on honesty and expect a lot from their prospective partners. They may be remarkable for their strength of character, but they also like to dominate.

Water tends to bring creativity to a sign. It is a compassionate element, and for those born under a sign whose subjects have a tendency to be caustic, if they have water as their element, this quality is diluted. Water also makes lovers yielding and easily influenced by their partners.

Wood and consideration go hand in hand; the element encourages warmth, generosity and cooperation. Those with wood as their element will usually try hard to see others' points of view.

Fire is the most dynamic of the five elements. When it is attached to a sign, the upside is that it encourages a sense of honor; the downside is that it can cause an inflexible and stubborn temperament.

Earth people are hard workers, especially in making others see their point of view. They are patient, especially in love. They're willing to wait for their affections to be returned, whereas other signs would give up and search elsewhere. Earth people can also be stubborn.

As with Western astrology, one of the main ways in which the Chinese put their beliefs into practice is to ascribe different personality traits to each sign, map out the future of those born under them, and see which signs are compatible in romantic matters and which should be avoided. What follows can only be extremely general, although the author (a Rooster) recognized something of himself in that section and he was more than a little impressed!

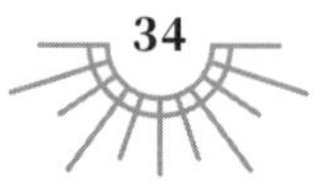

THE RAT

Charming, appealing, clever, quick-witted, and sociable, the Rat is regarded as wise. Their habit of scurrying around in the dark gave rise to the belief that they had occult powers. Rats, with their inquisitive nature, seem to want to know as much as they can about absolutely everything.

Those born under the sign speak and write with impressive fluency. They have a practical nature, and can turn their hand to most things. They are party animals and inveterate gamblers.

They have a deep-rooted fear of not being loved, which is why they play the field in romance. They are also afraid of running out of the money they need to finance their lifestyles, which is why they pack away money in savings accounts.

In matters of health, Rats' reliance on themselves can produce stress.

When it comes to sex and love, Rats can be obsessive and often form fiery relationships with Dragons. But when the passion dies down, Rats often find themselves seeking solace in the arms of a Pig or an Ox, with whom they often form long-lasting relationships. Rats can find themselves attracted to Horses and Monkeys, but the speed of the former and the capriciousness of the latter tend to ensure that the flames of passion are soon doused.

YEARS
1936
1948
1960
1972
1984
1996

THE OX

A dependable beast of burden, and to some a symbol of fertility, the Ox arrives early in the year, heralding spring.

People born in the year of the Ox are sometimes seen as slow, but they are intelligent and often concerned about the environment. They love their homes and need them to provide a stable base for themselves and their families.

Oxen can also be stubborn and sullen. Just as the animal will plow furrow after furrow, oblivious to distraction, those born under this sign wear blinders. And they can be possessive to the point of obsessiveness. They make excellent team workers and are unlikely to be accused of not pulling their weight. They are meticulous planners and can work late into the night; they remain miraculously full of energy the next day.

When it comes to trying to make sure that their relationships are well balanced, the Ox can become obsessive. Roosters and Dragons are happy to put up with, or even encourage, this. But Tigers and Pigs are usually far too aggressive for the Ox.

Oxen have a sweet tooth, and their tendency to overeat can cause problems. They are sensitive to extremes of temperature, which cause them discomfort in the stomach and chest.

YEARS
1937
1949
1961
1973
1985
1997

THE TIGER

Those born under the sign of the Tiger tend to be competitive and brave. They enjoy their charisma and, although they tend to be loners in some aspects of their lives, they see themselves as natural leaders and naturally superior. They can be among the most philanthropic of people, but whereas others do good by stealth, Tigers enjoy having their efforts noticed.

Conquest is the name of the game in business and in relationships. And they rarely fail.

Tigers can juggle a seemingly endless number of projects, managing several simultaneously and with ease. Others may see the Tiger as a menace, but not as much of a menace as the Tiger sees itself! It craves safety and finds it in its home, which is almost certain to be lavishly, some may even say ostentatiously, furnished.

When Tigers give their hearts, it is often to fellow felines who share their intensity. Problems can arise because of the Tiger's passivity in romance and tendency to be unfaithful. The one sign Tigers should avoid is the Pig—far too nervous to snuggle up to a big cat.

Tigers' overconfidence can make them take on far too much, which can cause symptoms of stress that the sleek animal often ignores until it is too late and the damage has been done.

THE RABBIT

Gregarious at times and wallflowers at others, Rabbits have an innate fear of getting involved. And when any sort of confrontation looms, they try to dig themselves into a burrow until it's gone. If you know someone who stays on the sidelines of social gatherings but is first on the phone for a good gossip, that's a Rabbit. They are the great breeders of the Zodiac menagerie: it's family first, and although they may roam far from home, they can't wait to scurry back to the warren—usually one they've lived in for a long time. If there's one thing a Rabbit hates, it's upheaval.

They have a wily intelligence, which they wield with great skill to get them out of sticky situations. They hoard things, and if you ask a Rabbit to go shopping, they will drop what they're doing and help you spend, spend, spend.

Rabbits make great friends and excellent business partners. Not the most sensual of animals, they relish long-term relationships with partners who will grow and mature alongside them. Rats and Oxen are the signs best suited to cope with the Rabbit's ways. Snakes will exhaust them emotionally, and fellow Rabbits are far too elusive to allow themselves to be snared.

THE DRAGON

To the Ancient Chinese, the Dragon crossed the skies and marked time's passing. A helpful creature blessed with vitality and occult powers, the Dragon marked auspicious events.

People born under this sign are blessed with that same vitality. Their ability to understand any situation puts them in a position to influence events. But that influence may be unwanted, which is often due to the fact that they have their heads in the clouds.

Dragons can believe they're infallible. They start projects and relationships with boundless enthusiasm, only to abandon them when their impetuosity drives them in another direction. Their superficial bravado often disguises insecurity, which they will go to great lengths to cover with a wide smile or a showy outfit.

They have so much energy that trying to channel it can become a preoccupation. This explains the frustration they feel when things don't go their way; it can cause volcanic outbursts.

Dragons need love and affection, which the Rooster and Snake are happy to offer. Surprisingly, the Tiger and the Dragon can be an excellent match. The Horse tends to be too devious, and Dragons attracted to a Dog will soon find that they are barking up the wrong tree.

YEARS

1940
1952
1964
1976
1988
2000

龙

THE SNAKE

Hypnotic and charming, wise but naïve, prudent, profligate, and possessive, with more than a touch of prudery thrown in. The word "contradiction" was invented for Snakes. They lie in wait until it's time to act. Those who see this as inactivity do so at their peril, for the Snake is planning the next move down to the last detail. Snakes gather intelligence with the same appetite with which a glutton attacks his food, then sieve it and put it in the right compartment of their intelligent minds. Facts may be their diet, but they also cook up original ideas, especially artistic ones. Sometimes their judgment might be unbalanced, and the solutions they come up with can be off-target. Not that the Snake will see this.

Their love of companionship encourages them to stay close to home. But their love of the creative arts can overcome this. They are the late risers of the Chinese Zodiac, often staying in bed when the rest of us are up. But the Snake is conserving its energy and planning its day.

In matters of romance, Snakes are well matched with the Dragons or Dogs. A Rat will play with a Snake's emotions and while the Tiger has its attractions, it is too prone to betrayal for the Snake to be truly comfortable.

YEARS

1941
1953
1965
1977
1989
2001

蛇

THE HORSE

Those born under the Horse are as sociable, hard-working and well-traveled as the animal itself. The downside? They can develop strong prejudices, becoming selfish and intolerant.

Their vitality and energy can drive them to do almost anything they set their mind to, leaving the rest of us at the starting post, watching with envy as luck smiles on them again and again. To the Horse, life is a game played constantly on the attack. The word "defense" is not in their vocabulary, but the word "winner" is—and that is what they strive to be.

But Horses are just as willing to use their strengths to help friends. They're team players as long as they can quell their desire to be coach. They take an overall view, leaving the details to others. That can lead to their downfall: charging forward, attention on the goalpost, they often fail to clear the details, which are hurdles in their path. And when things don't go according to plan, Horses will be just as hard on others as they are on themselves.

Horses are practical and handy to have around the house. When they settle down, it is often with the extrovert Tiger or the outgoing Dragon. Rarely will a Horse be happy with a Ram (too methodical) or a Monkey (too restless).

THE RAM

Rams are orderly creatures who like everything to be in its proper place. They are conservative, and believe that everything should be done only if the correct method can be found—and oh, the fear of failure if it can't. When Rams set themselves a target, it will be a realistic one.

Rams want things to run smoothly, not just for themselves, but for their friends and colleagues. They will move heaven and earth to ensure a trouble-free path through life, even if it seems a little interfering at times. A business that needs a methodical approach could do no better than look to a Ram for help. Rams are masters of the waiting game, only acting when they think the time is right. The word "inspiring" is not one that could be applied to most Rams, but when it comes to planning for the future, they are unparalleled. If you are on a tight deadline, don't ask a Ram for help.

They are home-loving creatures who like nothing more than throwing parties, not just because they enjoy hosting, but also because they like showing off their homes. They are happy with other Rams and with Horses, one of the few signs that can get through the Ram's reserve. Oxen are far too bovine for Rams, who are often attracted to Rats—but not for long.

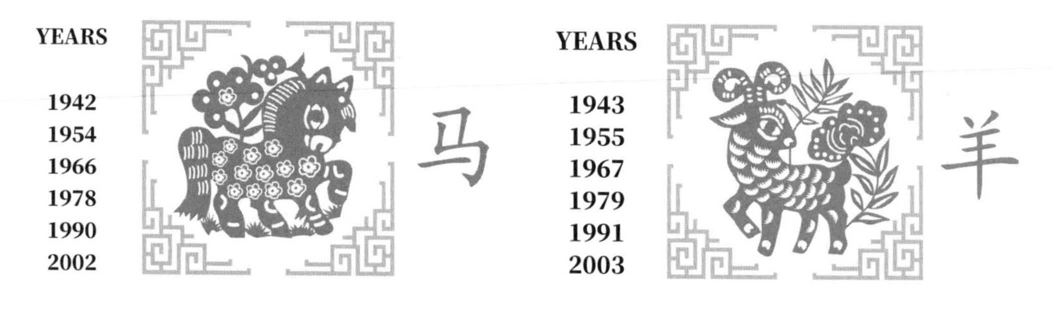

THE MONKEY

Watching a monkey in the wild, one can only wonder at their agility, audacity, and constant activity, all of which take a toll in the end. That's when they slump, exhausted and unmoving. It's the same with their Zodiac counterparts. Always on the go, inventive, and great fun to be with, they often have times when they feel insecure and depressed—but not for long. That irrepressible sense of fun soon re-emerges and they're off again, cajoling the rest of us to lighten up. They can be outrageously flirtatious and manipulative, but they really do love their fellows, and their intentions are usually good.

Don't be fooled by their madcap behavior. Monkeys know what they want, and usually get it. If they have to play games with people to do so, when they get caught, they are usually forgiven. They can be on the go for days, then slump, gather their energy and start again, fidgeting and interfering with other people's lives—usually for the common good, though.

Oxen will put up with Monkeys' hyperactivity, and the Rat makes a good partner, too, calming the Monkey and encouraging it to enjoy a little domesticity. Horses and Monkeys tap into the same energy source, but they will never settle down together—it's too exhausting a combo.

YEARS

1944
1956
1968
1980
1992
2004

THE ROOSTER

A natural leader, the Rooster is alert to new opportunities and is usually the first to see a problem arising. Others often see the Rooster crowing about their own achievements, abrasive and over-competitive—and they are right. But Roosters don't give a hoot. Sights set, they will get there—how is a minor consideration. Although in business they are taskmasters, Roosters are often selfless employers with the best interests of their employees at heart. Don't be fooled! The Rooster probably started the business, and is acting out of pure self-interest.

Watch a rooster in the coop. See how it struts among the chickens, enjoying the admiration. The Rooster is just the same. With their extravagant appearance and behavior, they shine at parties, especially if they have something new to show for their success.

The good-natured Pig is a good match for the Rooster and although the two will fight for dominance, harmony will soon replace aggression and they will make a devoted couple.

Roosters and Dogs don't make a good match—too distant. And although the Rabbit may seem like a good partner, it won't last; the Rooster's traits will annoy, and he will be surprised at how strongly the Rabbit reacts.

YEARS

1945
1957
1969
1981
1993
2005

THE DOG

Loyal, protective and fearless, the Dog lends all its characteristics to those born during its years of ascendancy in the Chinese Zodiac. They will get involved in things, often without thinking of the consequences. What they want is results, and they want them NOW! Not for them lengthy periods of negotiation or discussion.

Dogs are honest and straightforward, often with a seemingly placid nature that belies an underlying restlessness. They are steadfast in their friendships and make few enemies—but when they do, watch out! And being quick to show the affection they feel for others, they make it easy for them to feel quite unembarrassed when demonstrating the feelings they return. They are optimistic, sometimes overly so, which can result in disappointment. They simply don't understand it when a friendship goes awry, which is why they should sometimes sit back on their hindquarters and take stock.

Dogs and Tigers, perhaps surprisingly for seeming opposites, often enjoy passionate affairs and sizzling long-term relationships, but Pigs are probably the best match for Dogs. Rats are usually too nervous for the sociable canine and a match with an Ox is almost guaranteed to end in a battle of wills from which winner takes all.

YEARS

1946
1958
1970
1982
1994
2006

狗

THE PIG

Pigs are born at a time when new horizons beckon. They are creative and intelligent, and happy to take the world as they find it, something that explains the fact that the Pig is a contented animal. They use their intelligence for the benefit of others, because they are as generous as the day is long.

They often enjoy a lively social life, but at the end of the day they're equally happy to return to the sty. And therein lies a porcine problem.

They like their homes so much, they can become over-anxious about finding the right partner to share it with. And when that person doesn't show up, the Pig can become depressed. The family is central to Pigs and, while they are happy for their offspring to leave home and go their own way, when it comes to coming home for Sunday lunch whenever possible, there's a three-line whip in operation.

Pigs and Rabbits make a good match, with the latter's liveliness infecting the Pig to its advantage. And Dragons, as long as they can be persuaded to calm down and enjoy a quieter life than they are used to, make perfect partners for Pigs. Snakes and Pigs communicate on different wavelengths, and a Horse will unseat a Pig at the first opportunity.

YEARS

1947
1959
1971
1983
1995
2007

Table of Compatibility

	MOST COMPATIBLE	LEAST COMPATIBLE		MOST COMPATIBLE	LEAST COMPATIBLE
	Dragon Monkey Ox	Sheep Horse Rabbit		Tiger Sheep Dog	Rat Ox Rabbit
	Rat Snake Rooster	Horse Dog Sheep		Rabbit Horse Pig	Ox Dog
	Horse Dog	Snake Monkey		Rat Dragon Snake	Tiger Pig
	Sheep Pig Dog Rat	Dragon		Ox Dragon Snake	Rat Rabbit Dog
	Rat Monkey Rooster	Ox Rabbit Dog		Tiger Rabbit Horse Ox	Rooster Dragon
	Ox Rooster	Tiger Pig		Sheep Rabbit	Snake Monkey Pig

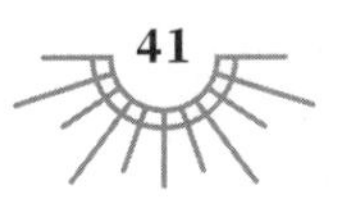

4

I Ching

Legend has it that around 5000 BCE, Fu Hsi, the first Chinese emperor, was meditating by a river when suddenly an animal that looked like a dragon rose from the water. Fu Hsi, curious rather than scared, noticed that there were lines on its scales.

Intrigued, he pondered these lines and after a while felt that they helped him by making him a wiser man. A man of spirited generosity, he felt that if the animal had helped him, it could help others, and set about drawing a series of diagrams, a series of broken and unbroken lines, using the lines on the scales as his guide.

Another tale credits the same man, and dates the incident to around the same time and the same place, but has it that the animal in question was a tortoise—tortoise shells being a common means of divination.

The lines that Fu Hsi noted were the eight trigrams—a stack of three lines, each of which have specific attributes to the Earth, Mankind and Heaven. As with all things Chinese, the Yin and the Yang exerted their profound influence—the unbroken lines representing Yang, that controls Heaven, the day's activities, the Sun's heat, action, and hardness. The broken lines are Yin, the feminine aspect that controls the Earth, the night's mystery, the cool Moon, softness, and stillness.

Whichever of these (and other legends) is true is irrelevant; what matters is that the lines became the basis of I (pronounced "ee") Ching, one of the most popular forms of divination in the East, and one that is currently increasing in popularity in the Western world.

Thousands of years later, around 1150 BCE, the tyrant emperor Chou Sin imprisoned "King" Wen, for what crime we do not know. But during his seven-year imprisonment, Wen refined the trigrams and devised the six-line hexagrams, or kua, and wrote a commentary for each.

COINS	VALUE	SYMBOL
3 tails	—o—	"Moving" Yang
3 heads	—x—	"Moving" Yin
2 tails/1 head	——	Yang
2 heads/1 tail	— —	Yin

While Wen was in prison, his eldest son, Yu, assembled an army and overthrew Chou Sin. Yu became emperor in his place, and bestowed on his father the title "King," a sobriquet by which he has been known ever since, even though he never ruled China.

When Yu died, he was succeeded by his brother Tan, the Duke of Chou, who had been thoroughly instructed in the I Ching by their father. It was he who interpreted the meaning of each line, and it was at this point, around 1100 BCE, that the I Ching was considered complete.

One of the earliest methods of using the I Ching was to heat a tortoise until its shell cracked, and then interpret the cracks that appeared! Thank goodness we have moved on since then, and today there is more than one method.

Traditionalists use yarrow sticks to cast the I Ching. This is hugely complicated and involves gathering fifty stalks of yarrow, one of which is set aside, and manipulating the remaining forty-nine stalks in four stages of operation. These four operations are repeated three times to form a line and, since there are six lines, 72 steps are required for the whole process. It is a time-consuming method.

Given the complexity of the yarrow method, it was inevitable that a simpler method of casting a hexagram would develop; today the most common way of casting a hexagram is to use coins—"the Heavenly Pennies." Some people strike a balance between the ultra-traditionalism of the yarrow and the upstart coins by using specially made I Ching stones, which are marked with either a Yin or a Yang symbol. Traditionalists need not worry. The means may vary, but the interpretation remains the same, harking back to Ancient China.

The method is simple. Take three coins and throw them down together, each throw forming a hexagram line.

Chinese coins were inscribed on one side only and had a hole in the middle so that they

could be threaded together. The inscribed side was Yin, and the plain side was Yang.

Modern coins are inscribed on both sides. For the purpose of the I Ching, the "tails" side is allied to the inscribed side and is therefore Yin; the "heads" side is assumed to be blank and is therefore "Yang."

CREATING THE HEXAGRAMS

These, then, are the basis of the sixty-four hexagrams, which are nowadays usually cast using coins. Before this is done, the question to be answered should be carefully framed in the mind. Most practitioners create a relaxing atmosphere, perhaps using mellow lighting and fragrant incense. The more particular the question, the more detailed the answer the I Ching will yield.

Only when the question has been thoroughly pondered should the coins be cast to create a hexagram, which is built from the bottom up. Very often, the answer to one question leads to another, but again, this should be thoroughly focused on before the second (and subsequent) hexagrams are created.

Take three coins of the same denomination. If they have no obvious "heads" or "tails," decide which side is which. The lines they create are shown on the table on page 45. The first throw gives the first line, the second throw the second line, and so on, until a six-line hexagram has been created. As the hexagram is being built, mark each line on a piece of paper. Initially, the moving lines are read as if they were ordinary Yin and Yang ones. But once the hexagram has been built, moving lines are reversed in meaning: a "Moving" Yin line becomes an unbroken Yang line, and a "Moving" Yang line becomes a broken Yin one.

Historically, changing lines have the following significance: a changing first line points to a problem or a change that cannot find a solid foundation. A changing second line indicates instability. The third line suggests change due to shifts in time that cannot have been foreseen. The fourth line can point to change brought about by another's involvement, while the fifth points to beneficial changes brought about by an advancement of some kind. And the sixth says that the situation regarding the question is currently unbalanced.

The I Ching, or *The Book of Changes*, the Chinese manuscript in which the meanings of the sixty-four hexagrams are explained, is a work of intense beauty. Each hexagram is described and explained line by line in the words of the philosopher. The most worthy translation is probably that of Richard Wilhelm and Cary F. Baynes, which was published by Princeton University Press in 1967. Space precludes us, in this book, from going into the hexagrams in the exquisite detail that was the luxury of Wilhelm and

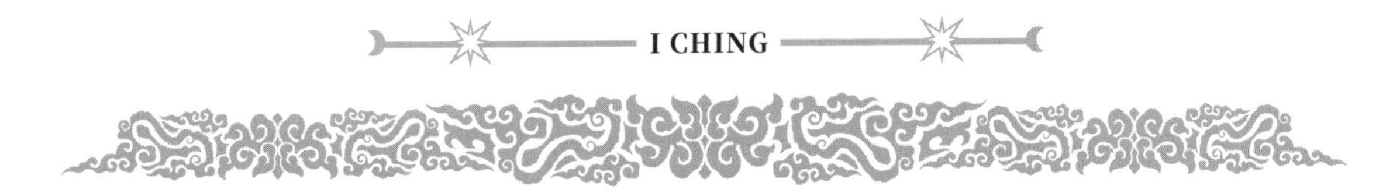

Baynes. Instead we shall restrict ourselves to a few key words about each of the sixty-four, and assure those who are drawn to the I Ching that it is well worth further study.

1. Chi' en—The Creative

Success is assured through the questioner's strength, power, and persistence. Plans can be continued with confidence, as long as there is no overreaching or overstretching of resources.

2. K' un—The Receptive

The future can be viewed with confidence, as things will happen, but in their own time. And as success may lie in other people's hands, the questioner is advised to be still, responsive, and receptive to advice.

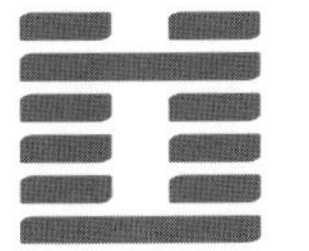

3. Chun—Initial Difficulty

Opportunities that present themselves should be viewed with care, as they might spell danger. If help is needed, don't be afraid to ask for it. And since it's early days, take care; there's no need to act hastily.

4. Meng—Innocence

There may be a lack of experience, or even wisdom, so listen to the advice of other, more worldly people and learn from it. Remain enthusiastic and don't give up, whatever you do.

5. Hsu—Waiting

Patience is a virtue. After all, if you plant seeds in a field, you don't expect to harvest them right away. Help will be at hand when the time is right, so don't force the pace and worry. Wait and be ready.

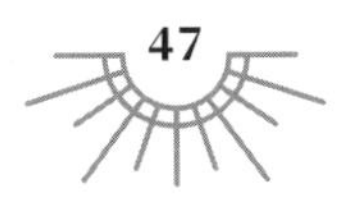

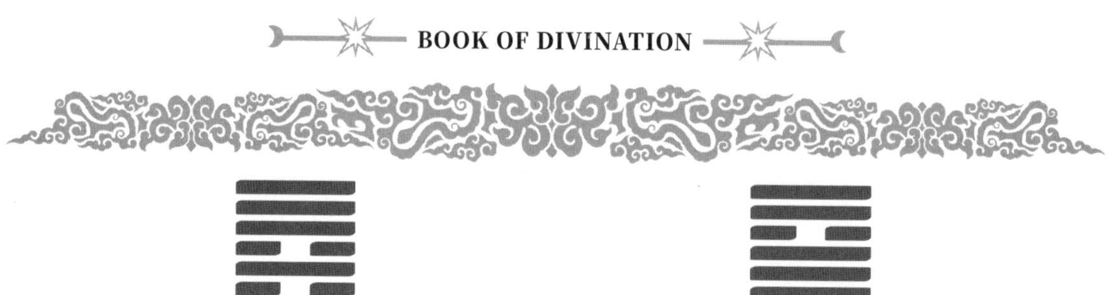

6. Sung—Connection

Compromise is the keyword at the moment. Impulsive action, arguments, and aggressive behavior are to be avoided. If criticism is offered, accept it. Listen to advice and things will improve.

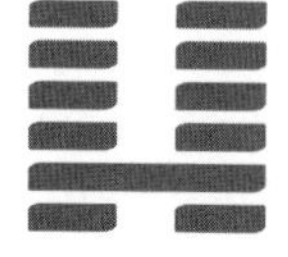

7. Shih—The Arrow

Ask for respect and it will be received. If promotion is desired, it will come, but after a struggle and probably after receiving some good advice from a wiser, and generally more mature, person.

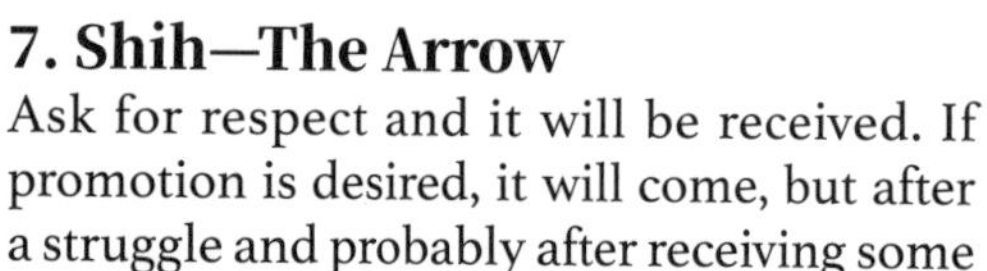

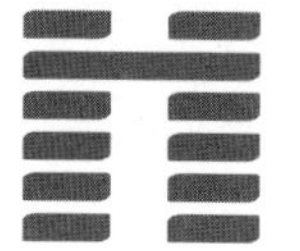

8. Pi—Union

This is the time to build strong bonds by sharing experiences with others. Help them and at the same time you will be helping yourself. Pi is also an indication of harmonious partnerships.

9. Hsiao Ch' u—Taming Force

Now is the time to use your strength and power to clear small blockages from your path so that you are ready for the future. And although times may be hard, be thankful for small mercies. Restraint may be called for.

10. Luí—Treading Carefully

Stick to the path you have chosen, and press forward without hesitating.

11. T' ai—Tranquility

Good fortune and harmony are all around, so enjoy them and share them with others. This is a good time for planning for the future and for steady progress, but beware the temptation to act rashly.

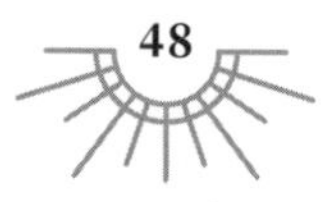

12. P' I 1—Stagnation

This is not the time to force the pace, even if you are sure that there are rewards to be had. Modesty is called for if the change in the air is to be turned to your advantage.

13. T' ung Jen—Companionship

There are rewards to be had from working with others as long as everyone sticks to the tasks that have been allotted to them. This is a time for sharing. It is also a time when travel is indicated.

14. Ta Yu—Great Possession

Work hard and save for the future, and success is yours for the taking.

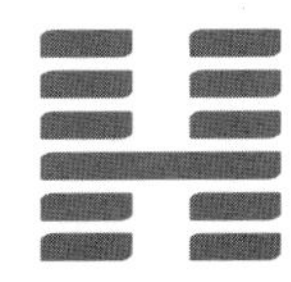

15. Ch' ien 2—Humility

Be modest and others will give you the help you need. Harmony is everything, and it is vital to remain tolerant of others no matter how bad their behavior may appear to be.

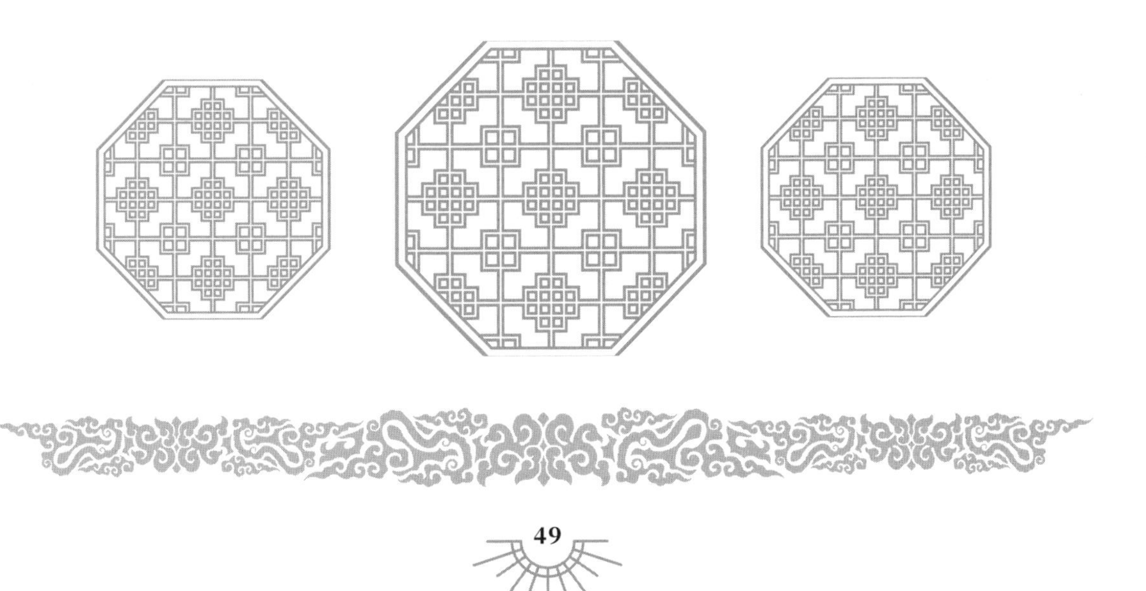

16. Yu—Happiness

Sell yourself, without necessarily believing what you say. This is a good time to plan for the future, but remember that money isn't everything; spiritual health is just as important as a bulging wallet.

17. Sui—Following

Now is the time to take a back seat and let others take charge. Be as flexible as you can and avoid any conflict. Take a relaxed view of things, but without letting your goals slip from view.

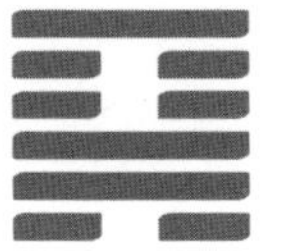

18. Ku—Disruption

Honesty is the best policy, so think hard and when you move forward, do so with care. If you have made mistakes in the past, now is the time to rectify them.

19. Lin—Approach

Let caution be your watchword, move forward with care and consider the feelings of others more than you may have in the past. Rash decisions are especially costly at the moment, and may make today's good fortune temporary.

20. Kuan—Observing

This is a good time to plan for the future and look beneath the surface of things. Joint ventures could pay unexpected dividends, especially if you watch, listen, and learn.

21. Shih Ho—Biting Through

Be positive about the success that has been achieved. And don't let the negativity of others affect you. There may be a legal matter of some kind to deal with, but you can win—in other areas, too.

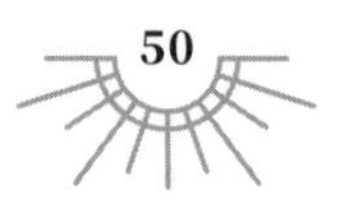

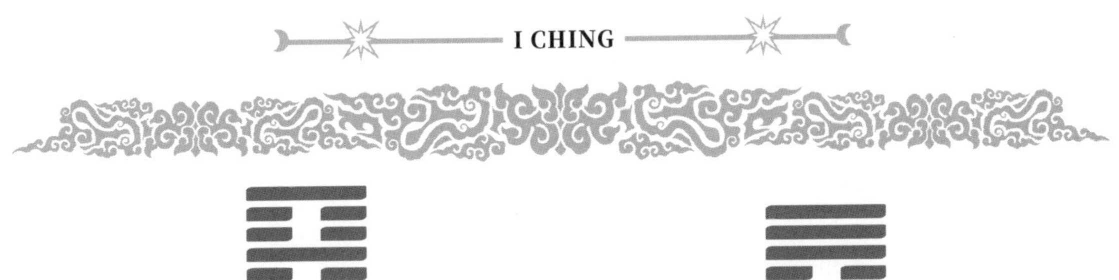

22. P' I 2—Adornment

Keep a rein on spending, especially if you are trying to create an impression. There are probably things that need to be figured out, but do so in small stages, for the time is not right for sweeping changes.

23. Po—Stripping Away

This is not the time for action, for the odds are not in your favor. There are disruptions ahead and change in the air. So wait, and do what is needed to cope with them.

24. Fu—Returning

Caution, particularly regarding anything new, is the watchword at the moment. It is a time for patience and for timing the path ahead. It also indicates that old energies will be refreshed and new ones appear.

25. Wu Wang—Correctness

Remember that everything has its limits—don't be tempted to go beyond them. Selflessness and simplicity are keywords at the moment. Remember that problems are usually of a temporary nature, so be ready for the time when they vanish.

26. Ta Ch' u—Taming Force

Work is hard and progress slow, but luck is on your side and success is on the way, especially if you learn from mistakes made in the past.

27. I 1—Nourishment

Take care not only about what you eat and drink, but also what you say. This is a time to build strength, bide your time, and keep ambitions very much in check.

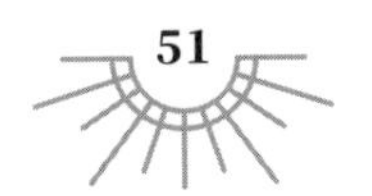

28. Ta Kuo—Excess

This is a time for extraordinary action. The inner voice should be listened to. And success is there, waiting for you to grasp it.

29. K' an—The Deep

Take care and be on the lookout for pitfalls. Conflict is in the air. Proceed with caution, but make sure that you do proceed. Have faith in yourself and all will be well.

30. Li—Fire

Success can often be had by recognizing one's limitations. Now is the time to put the intellect to use, and to be calm but firm.

31. Hsein—Sensitivity

Be receptive to other people's ideas and try to keep feelings of envy at arm's length. Help others at every opportunity, but do so for genuine reasons, and don't try to rule the roost at the expense of someone else.

32. Heng—Persistence

Set your course and stay with it. Stick to traditional methods and avoid any rash behavior. If others offer advice, listen to it.

33. Tun—Withdrawal

There may be trouble ahead, but if you judge the right time to withdraw from the situation, and you are practical, you will weather the storm.

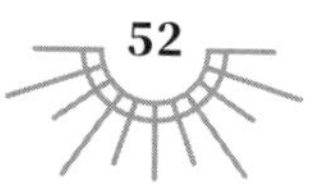

34. Ta Chuang—The Power of Greatness

If you say something, be sure that you stick to what you promise. This is a time of good fortune. If you act wisely, you will benefit from it.

35. Chin—Advancement

This is a time when honesty is the best policy, and also a time to think of others. Do so and there is promotion or/and social advancement in your future.

36. Ming I—Darkening of the Light

Try not to get bogged down by making too many plans. Keep to the few that you have, and try not to get too down in the mouth if things go badly. They will soon get better.

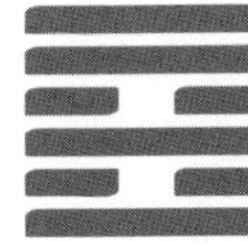

37. Chia Jen—Family

Family matters are to the fore, and it will probably be necessary to exercise authority. But try to do so fairly and with tolerance. Men may find that the wisest course of action is to let their partners take the wheel for the time being.

38. K' uei—Opposition

Try to stay in tune with the Yin and the Yang by ironing out anything disruptive or inharmonious in your life. It is a good time for starting small projects, and remember that mighty oak trees grow from tiny acorns.

39. Chien 1—Halting

There are hard times ahead, with problems on the horizon. The only way to solve them is to face them. Do so without making a song and dance; just think about them.

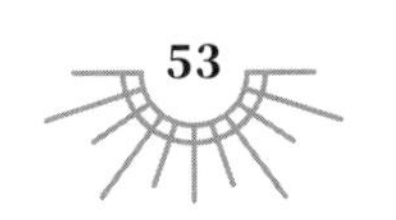

40. Chieh 1—Removing Obstacles

It's time for action, but not in haste. Solve the problem facing you, put it behind you, and move on with things, resisting the temptation to dwell on the past.

41. Sun 1—Decrease

Cut back on spending, but share what you have with others, even if it means making sacrifices in one area of your life. If you do this willingly, the gain will be yours in the end.

42. I 2—Increase

Luck is on your side, and you can make plans with confidence that they will be successful. You may make mistakes, but worry not. They will turn out to be to your benefit.

43. Kui—Breakthrough

Take precautions against possible losses and they will be kept to a minimum. Be firm without being pushy, and try to cultivate friends, for they will blossom.

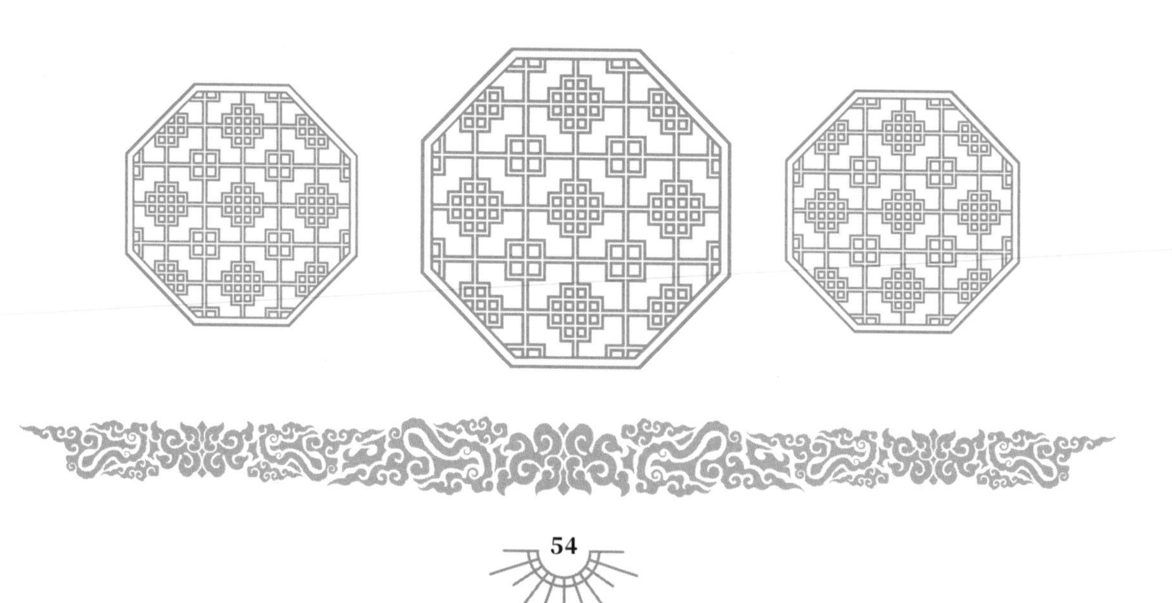

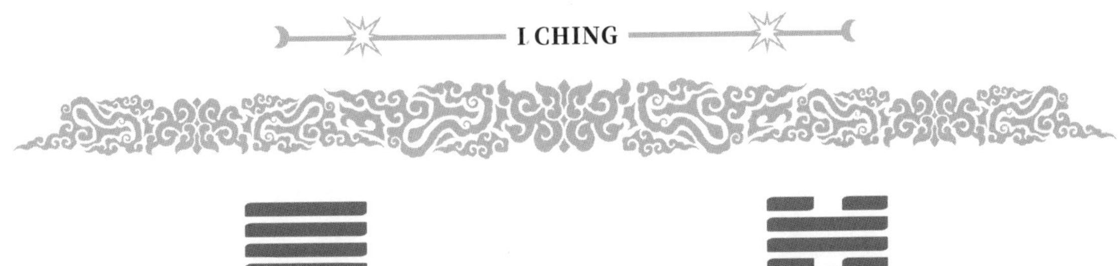

44. Kou—Meeting

Be resolute. Stand your ground and don't give in, whatever you do. Now is not the time to sign contracts or make agreements.

45. Ts' ui—Gathering Together

Sincerity and openness will help you make your relationship especially harmonious now. Keep a guard on your tongue. There may be a bit of a struggle ahead, and if you feel that you are on your own with regard to a project, it is best to ask just one person to help.

46. Sheng—Ascending

Be warned that although progress might be on the slow side, at least you are going forward, not in reverse. Professional help could be beneficial at the moment, which can generally be regarded as a good time.

47. K' un 2—Repression

Things are probably looking hard, but stay calm, composed, and as silent as possible, and you will cope, although you may have to dig deep into your reserves and be very determined to do so.

48. Ching—The Well

Things are looking up, but nothing lasts forever! Insincerity on your part could have disastrous consequences. Excellent judgment regarding a situation or another person may be called for now. It is a time to watch your guard.

49. Ko—Change

Big changes beckon regarding opportunities, followed by a series of smaller ones. Be alert, and remember that sometimes it pays to dress the part. Remember, too, that material things are not the only ones that matter in life.

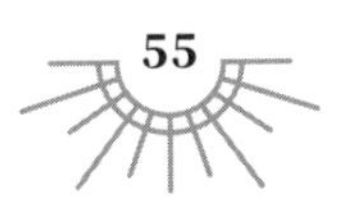

50. Ting—The Cauldron

You may find that lots of little things conspire to get you down at the moment: equipment goes wrong, plans run late. It's nothing serious, though. Life soon picks up, and things start to go well again, heralding further success. Don't forget to keep the material and spiritual parts of your life in balance.

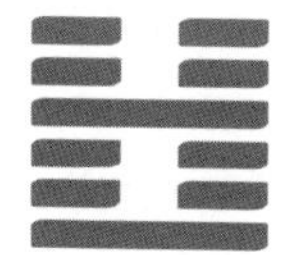

51. Chen—Thunder

The road ahead is rocky, but stay as calm as you can; it smooths out before too long. You may be about to hear some shocking news, though. Try not to let it affect you too much—it could be nothing more than tongues wagging.

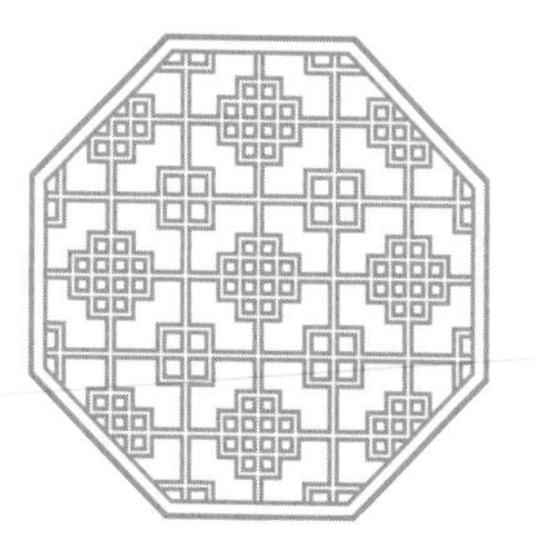

52. Ken—Mountain

If you maintain a low profile, problems that loom may well pass you by. Avoid taking risks. If you enjoy meditating, this is a good time for it; if you have never tried it, this is the best time to start.

53. Chien 2—Growth

"Softly, softly catchy monkey" is a good motto for the time being. Deal with things as they crop up, and don't try to force the pace, whatever you do.

54. Kuei Mei—Marrying Maiden

You could have been aiming too high; trim your sails and you won't regret it. Don't overdo things. And remember that it's always darkest before the dawn.

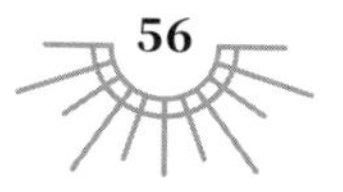

55. Feng—Abundance

Good fortune and good luck beam at you. Worries will soon be a thing of the past—for a time, at least.

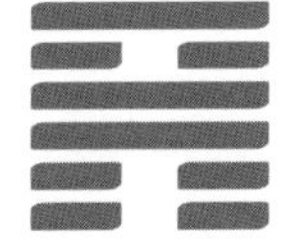

56. Lu 2—Travel

Movement and moving are on the cards. And with the changes this will bring, long-term commitments should be avoided. This is a time to make friends, but to choose them wisely.

57. Sun 2—Gentle

"Go with the flow," as they say, and be flexible. You might find that help comes from an unexpected source, so stick to any plans you have made, but do so without sticking your head too far above the parapet.

58. Tui—The Joyous

Good news and good fortune come your way. And your behavior makes people see just how in tune you are with your spiritual side. You could be asked to enter into a partnership. Work with the people who make the offer.

59. Huan—Dispersal

This is a time for reason, to take the middle path, for any other one could lead to failure of some kind. Friends from the past could resurface; if they do, strong spiritual bonds may be formed with them.

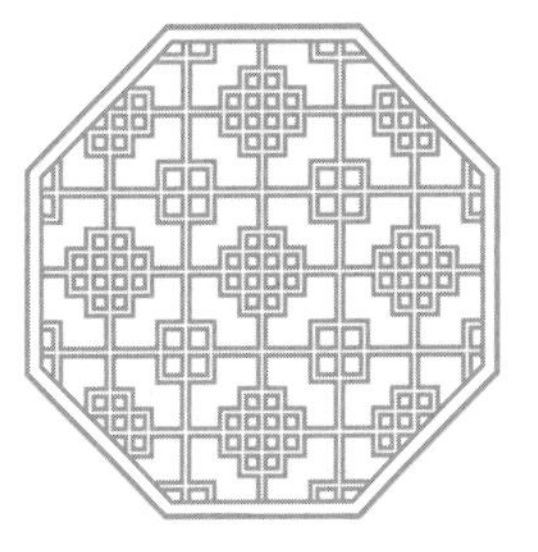

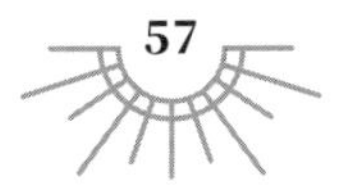

60. Chieh 2—Restraint

You will probably be feeling shackled in some way, but if you remain calm you will soon be free and ready to take advantage of new opportunities that will present themselves. This is also a good time to work toward becoming more self-aware.

61. Chung Fu—Innermost Sincerity

Favored results should come from properly judged communications. Plans made now for the future will certainly flourish.

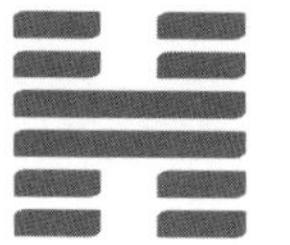

62. Hsiao Kua—Great Smallness

Success doesn't need to come in one big package; lots of small ones can be just as rewarding. If you are involved in any legal matters, remember that the devil is in the detail, so read the small print.

63. Chi Chi—Completion

Resist the temptation to rest on your laurels just because you have achieved some success. This is a good time to reinforce the gains you have made, and consolidate. Small matters need your attention.

64. Wei Chi—Before Completion

Don't make a move until you are certain the time is right, and even then proceed with caution. Think long and hard before getting involved in something new; you could come to regret it later, for there may be things of which you are unaware—important things.

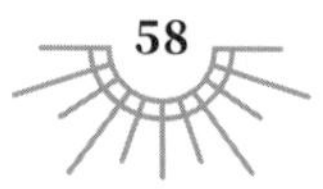

I CHING HEXAGRAMS TABLE
THE 64 SYMBOLS OF THE CHINESE BOOK OF CHANGES

UPPER TRIGRAM → / LOWER TRIGRAM ↓	☰	☳	☵	☶	☷	☴	☲	☱
☰	01	34	05	26	11	09	14	43
☳	25	51	03	27	24	42	21	17
☵	06	40	29	04	07	59	64	47
☶	33	62	39	52	15	53	56	31
☷	12	16	08	23	02	20	35	45
☴	44	32	48	18	46	57	50	28
☲	13	55	63	22	36	37	30	49
☱	10	54	60	41	19	61	38	58

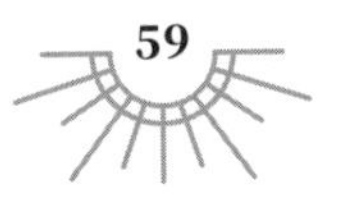

5

Numerology

Pythagoras, the founder of geometry, asserted that numbers were the essence of all things. Each one, he taught the students at his school in Crotone, Italy, had a unique vibration and personality. And it was he who divided the human soul into nine different types.

There is also a symbiotic connection between numbers and astrology, which has been with us for centuries. Each astrological sign is assigned a planet and a corresponding number, which, it can be assumed, have similar attributes.

For historical reasons, the Sun and the Moon are allocated two numbers because, when the system was devised, there were only seven known planets, and nine numbers to be allocated.

Numerology is concerned only with the numbers one to nine, to which all other numbers are reduced. Zero is not a number in numerology terms. It adds nothing at the beginning of a sequence and adds nothing to any other digit to which it is attached. The number ten exists as a composite of the number one (1 + 0 = 1). All subsequent numbers are treated in the same way.

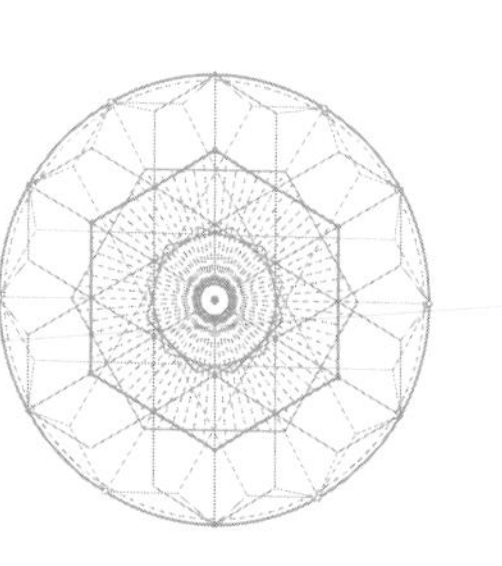
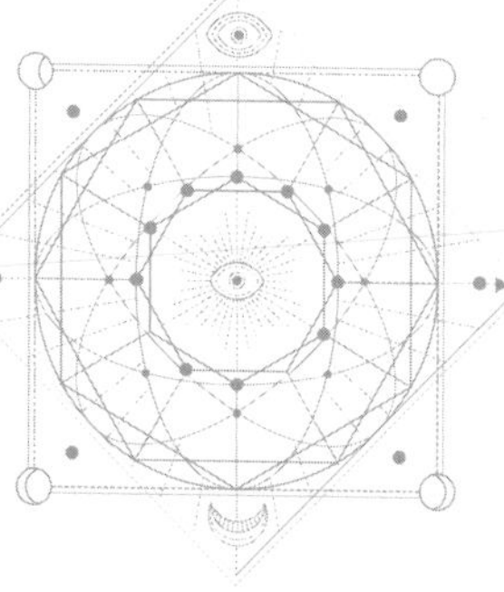
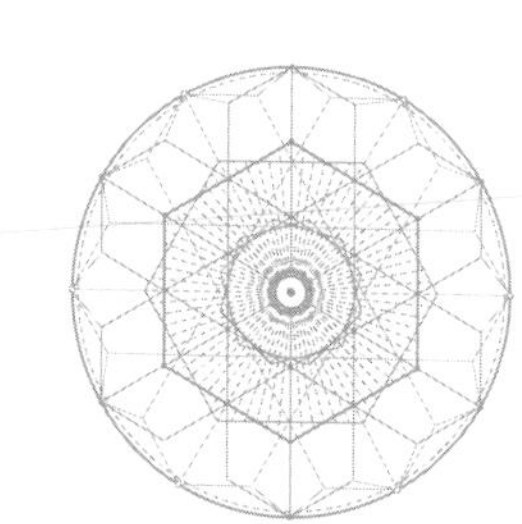

STAR SIGN	RULING PLANET	NUMBER
Aries	Mars	9
Taurus	Venus	6
Gemini	Mercury	5
Cancer	Moon	2/7
Leo	Sun	1/4
Virgo	Mercury	5

STAR SIGN	RULING PLANET	NUMBER
Libra	Venus	6
Scorpio	Mars	9
Sagittarius	Jupiter	8
Capricorn	Saturn	9
Aquarius	Saturn	8
Pisces	Jupiter	3

The Birth Number

This is the number that reveals natural powers and abilities. It is often used as an indication of likely career choices. To calculate this number, the individual components of the subject's date of birth are written down and then reduced to a single number. Thus, a person born on November 16, 1945 would have a birth number of 1, calculated as follows:
1 + 1 + 1 + 6 (November is the eleventh month) + 1 + 9 + 4 + 5 = 28.

Being a composite number, 28 is broken down to 2 + 8 = 10

And 10, being a composite number, is broken down to 1 + 0 = 1.

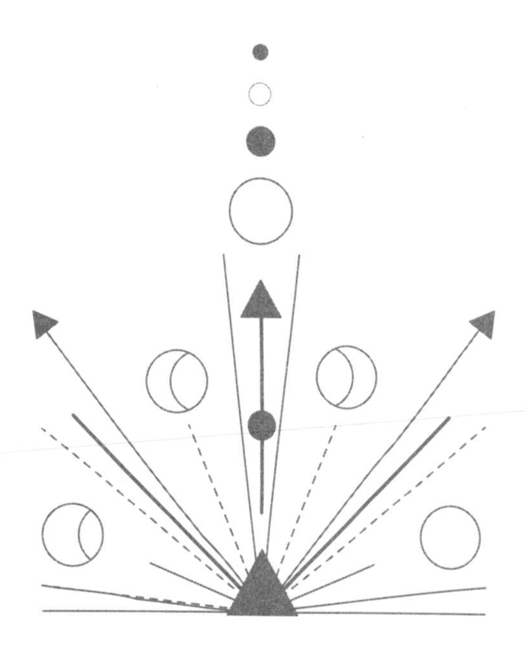

The associations of this number with the Sun and the Fire signs Leo, Sagittarius, and Aries, spell leadership. In many religions, it is the number of resurrection and, being the first number, rising from the chaos of nothing, it is linked with new beginnings, breaks with the past, and limitless energy. It is often linked with assertiveness and masculinity.

People whose birth number is one often have fair hair, an athletic body, and beautiful skin. They give off an aura of good health and wellbeing, and are usually perceived to be physically attractive with aesthetically pleasing features. The overall impression created by those with this number is one of action, fitness, and general good health.

But, being a young number, one can bring immaturity and a tendency to sulkiness, especially toward those who spurn attempts to be led. One people need loyalty, and when they don't get it, they feel slighted.

Linked to the Moon, now a symbol of femininity, two brings strong intuition, the power of deep thought, and attractive sensitivity. Men with two as their birth number are often in touch with their feminine side, and twos of both sexes are often fair-skinned with pale hair and a dislike of bright sunshine. They may be slender and show a tendency to underestimate themselves, something that leads to them having difficulty standing their ground.

They are often so quietly spoken that one has to strain to hear what they say. But they have a tendency to say one thing and do another, something that often causes difficulties in maintaining relationships.

Three is a mystical number in many cultures, as witnessed by the Holy Trinity. Chinese philosophers believed three was the number from which creatures that embraced the Yin and the Yang were created. Threes are usually uncommonly intelligent and wise; they love life and have a strong sense of the sensual.

Threes have outgoing personalities and share a dislike of their own company. They often have psychic abilities and love acquiring knowledge.

Four is another Sun number, which in many cultures is symbolized by the serpent. Fours often have a tough, aggressive nature, but keep it hidden under the well-balanced façade they present to the world. They enjoy hard work and the rewards it brings. They have tough bodies and quick, alert minds, but are often diffident when it comes to starting relationships because of a curious lack of confidence. But make friends with a four and you have a friend for life. That said, remember the dragon that lurks beneath the surface, and be careful not to stir it.

Five is the number of the planet Mercury, messenger to the gods and child of Maia, after whom the fifth month, May, is named. Fives are mentally and physically always on the move. They are often slender and find it hard to gain weight, due to the effect their constant hurrying and scurrying has on their fast metabolism.

They have persuasive tongues, especially when it comes to sex; they can charm the birds off the trees, and whoever they set their sights at into bed. Although they might be cheerful extroverts, they can be anxious and impatient. Also, their incessant movement often disguises prevarication; actually getting things done is quite different from looking busy.

Their agile minds make fives good inventors. Their fertile imaginations make them good authors. Their behavior may suggest genius, but it might just as easily suggest delusion. That's the trouble with fives. As Bernard Shaw wrote, "You never can tell, sir, you never can tell."

Venus's number, six, is the symbol of partnership, love, and marriage. Those whose birth number it is can be fairly certain that they will enjoy loving and fruitful relationships.

With their attractive, bright eyes, six people have pleasing manners, and are outgoing and friendly. But they can also be curiously introverted and enjoy the company of quiet, artistic people. They are home-loving people who enjoy looking good, something that can make them appear overdressed.

There are seven days in the week, seven colors in the rainbow, seven pillars of wisdom, and seven branches on a menorah. Seven is perhaps the most magical of the nine single-digit numbers with which numerology is concerned.

Seven people, though, are not so magical by nature. They are realists who are not preoccupied with appearance and superficiality, but instead prefer to cultivate a warm and cheerful disposition.

Sevens are often very friendly and make great company. They enjoy nothing more than seeing others enjoy themselves as much as they do.

With Saturn as its associated planet, eight is the number of secret, dark places.
It is symbolic of the good aspects of old age—wisdom and patience—and the unfortunate ones—regret, disillusionment, and failing health.

People whose birth number is eight are often tall and slender. Not that you will notice, for smiling is not something that Saturnine eights are prone to do often.

They mature earlier than their peers, something that makes them liable to express their opinions in an overly forthright way. But the strong ideals that they have, and their strong principles, often encourage others to seek their advice, something that will be given in the cold, dispassionate way that is typical of the eight person.

Mars, god of war, rules nine, the number of wisdom and virtue, and their opposites, ignorance and profligacy.

Nine people often have powerful physiques, ruddy complexions and dark hair. They tend to have facial hair and birthmarks.

Coming before ten, which reduces to one, nine rekindles the life spark. This makes nines confident, often overconfident, which is something that can lead to their being impetuous and accident-prone. And while they can be full of vitality and enthusiasm, ambitious and energetic, they can also be insecure and quarrelsome, slapdash and autocratic.

The Destiny Number

This number shows life's purpose, the opportunities that will present themselves, and how they should be used to achieve optimum potential. In calculating the Destiny Number, each letter of the full birth name is ascribed a number. These are then added together and treated as above until a single number is reached. Thus, someone named Michael Mitchell Johnstone at birth would calculate his Destiny Number as follows:
4 + 9 + 3 + 8 + 1 + 5 + 3 + 4 + 9 + 2 + 3 + 8 + 5 + 3 + 3 + 1 + 6 + 8 + 5 + 1 + 2 + 6 + 5 + 5 = 109 = 1 + 0 + 9 = 10 = 1 + 0 = 1

The name can also be used for more refined readings. By reducing the numerical values of just the vowels of any name to a single numeral, we get a number (the Name Vowel Number) that gives an indication that some say represents the Freudian ego—the exposed, conscious, outer self. Correspondingly, the Name Consonant Number, calculated using only the numerical values of the consonants, represents the Freudian id—the hidden, unconscious self.

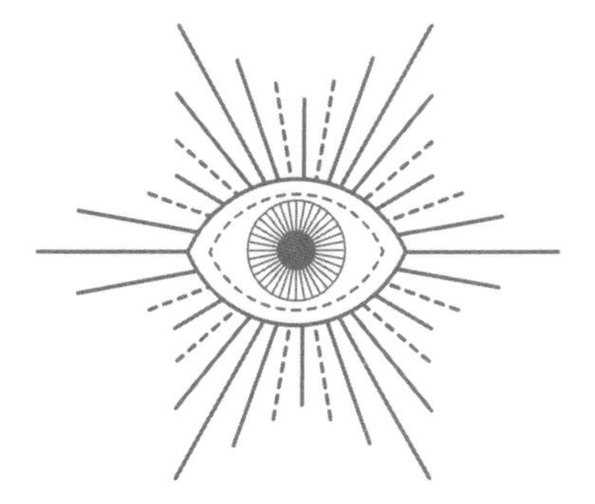

NAME VOWEL NUMBERS

Suggests an open, confident personality, but perhaps someone who genuinely believes themselves to be better than their fellows. If this goes unchecked, it might lead to selfishness and a tendency to offer the hand of friendship only to fawning acolytes. But ones are a gregarious group who make friends easily and enjoy money.

Often indicates a lack of self-confidence and a tendency to be, perhaps, a little too laid back, but it also hints at great creative talents. If twos can get their act together, they often make excellent counselors and caring members of the medical profession.

Points to a confident, extroverted nature, to people who enjoy the good things in life so much that they overindulge in them. Those with three as their Name Vowel Number are frank and honest to the point of bluntness. They are natural teachers with a thirst for learning, especially about the arts.

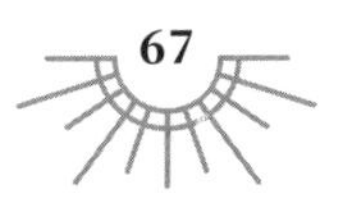

Says "responsibility," "dependability," and "stability," but also "self-doubt." Four people claim to like freedom in their friendships and their jobs, but deep down they harbor a desire for a more structured existence. Emotionally, they tend to keep to themselves. Professionally, they tend toward careers in the arts, architecture, and design.

Is often the Name Vowel Number of clever, quick-minded people who enjoy learning languages and acquiring new skills. They may have quick tempers and be obsessive about cleanliness and punctuality. They keep emotional commitments at bay, but love to gossip.

Is a number that suggests a well-balanced nature, perhaps a little reserved, and maybe a little over-polite. Those with this number are upset by anything that is controversial, untidy, or unjust. They may sit on the fence, seeing both sides of any argument, secretly longing to come down heavily in favor of one side, but holding back.

Encourages a bright, creative nature enjoyed by the sort of person who is always on the go, bouncing here, there, and everywhere, and with a deep desire to please everyone at the same time. They can be intellectual but erratic, often starting ambitious schemes only to drop them when the first hurdle looms.

Indicates a conventional nature, someone who is stable and cautious, but with a lively imagination that occasionally shows itself in behavior that surprises. People with this number don't like sudden change. They are often regarded as slow-moving, but they usually succeed in getting what they want, then move on to something else.

Is a pugnacious Name Vowel Number, often that of the sort of person who sees things in black and white, with no shades of gray. They act first and think later, but their enthusiasm and generosity often make those affected by their rash decisions forgive them quickly.

NAME CONSONANT NUMBERS

1

Suggests a strong sense of one's own worth and the belief that one's own ideas are always the best on offer.

Indicates a prolific imagination and the tendency to live in a fantasy world.

Points to a sensual nature and a feeling that one's deeply held religious or psychic beliefs set one apart from one's fellows.

Says that a creative nature is married to common sense, but warns that persistence might be mistaken for donkey-like stubbornness.

May make those with this number restless and eccentric, which some may find appealing and others unbelievably annoying.

Is a contemplative number, suggesting a liking for the meditative and the mystical, and a dislike of change.

Is associated with an instinctive knowledge of how things are and how they should be, and a liking for one's own company.

Speaks of caution, an unwillingness to take risks, and a dislike of waste. But it also has hints of sexual passion.

Is a number of deep desires—often, unfortunately, coupled with an inability to express them, which can lead to dashed ambitions and unrealized dreams.

6

Palmistry

Palmistry is the marriage of two ancient disciplines—chirognomy, which studies the shape, texture, color, and markings of the human hand, and what they tell us about a person's character; and chiromancy, which aims to use the information the hand holds to divine future events.

Like so much of divination, palmistry was first practiced in China more than 3,000 years ago (where it was, and remains, part of a larger attempt to see the identity of the "correct path" by scrutinizing not just the hand but also the face and forehead), and in India, where it is closely linked to astrology.

Aristotle taught the ancient art of chirosophy (*xier* = the hand and *sophia* = wisdom) to Alexander the Great, who at one point had a large part of the civilized world in the palm of his hand.

In 315 CE, six hundred years after Alexander died, a papal decree threatened excommunication or, in extreme cases, death to anyone "outside the Church," who practiced palmistry. It was officially frowned upon during the reign of Henry VIII (r. 1509-47). As late as the reign of George IV (r. 1820-30) it was decreed by Parliament that "Any person found practicing palmistry is hereby deemed a rogue and a vagabond, to be sentenced to one year's imprisonment and to stand in the pillory."

In Victorian times, it came to be regarded almost as a science, and was popular in upper-class salons, middle-class parlors, and working-class kitchens. Oscar Wilde used palmistry as the theme of one of his stories, "Lord Arthur Saville's Crime," in which, during a party, a palm reader tells the young Lord Arthur that he is destined to commit murder. He does. At the end, driven to distraction by his fate, he kills the man who determined it.

Carl Jung, the psychologist who studied introversion and extroversion, was fascinated by palmistry, and his followers came to believe that the

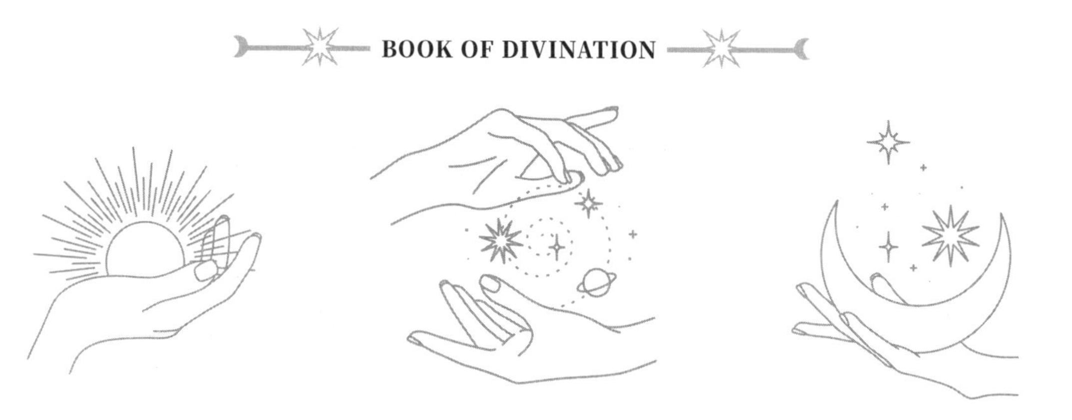

outward personality (the extrovert) is in the dominant hand and the inner one (the introvert) in the minor hand. The dominant hand reflects events that have happened and that are unfolding now—achievements and disappointments, changes of opinion—with the three main lines (heart, head, and life) representing the physical organs of the body. The minor hand can provide excellent insight into the subject's potential and what, deep down, they really want in life.

In this hand, the heart, head, and life lines signify the energies, nervous and sexual, that drive the subject.

Palmistry, like so much of divination, depends on two things: trust between the palmist and the subject, and instinct. The reading should take place in a relaxed atmosphere rather than in a tent at the county fair! A shaded room perfumed with suitable essential oils is ideal.

An introductory chat can tell the palmist a great deal about the subject: which is the dominant hand; whether the subject gesticulates as he or she talks; whether the hands are open and relaxed, or tense, with the fingers clenched into a fist; whether the fingers are adorned with rings. During this time, the reader might take the opportunity of taking the subject's hand, looking at the texture, the color, the condition of the fingernails, blemishes and, finally, one of the most important aspects of palmistry: the shape of the hand.

The actual reading can be done by examining the hand physically or by taking a palm print. Either way, the hands being studied must be washed and thoroughly dried and free of rings.

To make a palm print (one for each hand) you will need:

1. Acrylic print-making ink (available from craft and art-supply stores).
2. A smooth metal or glass surface on which to roll out the ink.
3. A hard rubber roller (available from craft and art-supply stores).
4. Glossy paper.

Squeeze some ink onto the smooth surface and push the roller back and forth until it is evenly coated. Roll the roller over the hand to be printed, then position a piece of glossy paper on a soft or rubbery surface and carefully press the hand onto it. Now roll the hand off the paper toward the edge, so that the edge of the hand, as well as the palm, is printed. The subject may need to be reassured that the ink comes off with soap and water.

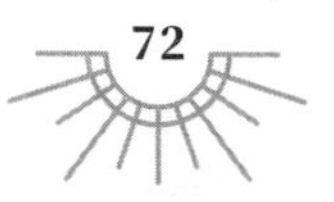

Types of Hands

Just as no two people, not even identical twins, have identical fingerprints, no two people have exactly the same hands. That said, it is possible to identify six basic types of hand that tell a great deal about the subject of the reading.

1. The normal or practical hand

This tends to be on the clumsy side, with fingers that are short in comparison with the palm. People with this type of hand often lack patience and are quick to lose their temper. They also tend to be among the most passionate.

2. The square or elemental hand

People who tend to be logical and, perhaps, creatures of habit often have square hands. They are also usually very helpful individuals who can be relied on in times of crisis. They are persistent to the point of doggedness, conventional, always above suspicion—and very often boring!

3. The spatulate hand

The hand and fingers of this type represent a fan, which indicates restlessness and excitability—the sort of person who can go from one extreme to another in the blink of an eye. Such people are often inventive, with an original view of the world that enables them to make discoveries. They are risk-takers and good company, but can be slapdash and have a tendency to bend the rules more than it is wise to do.

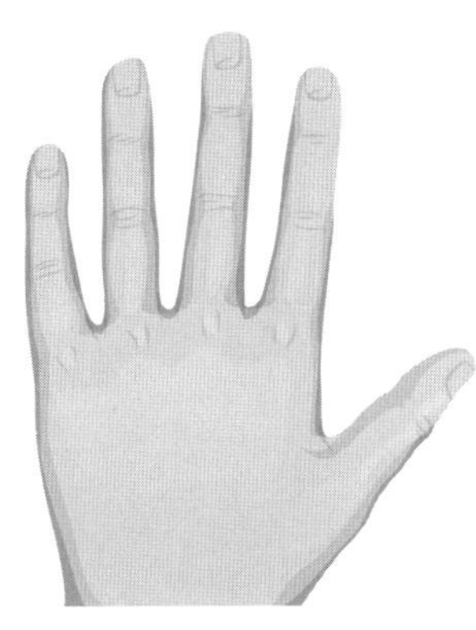

The normal or practical hand

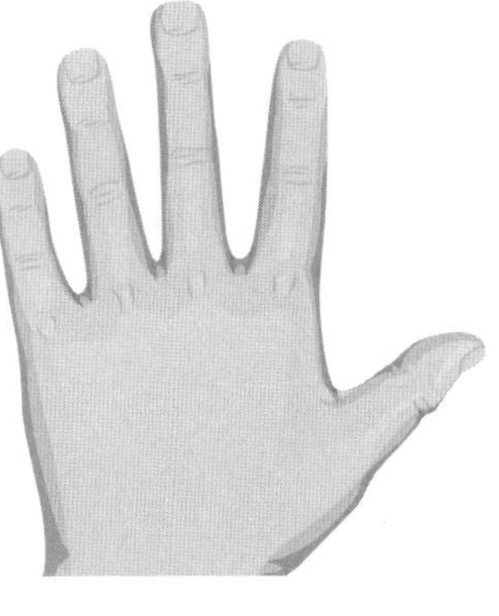

The square or elemental hand

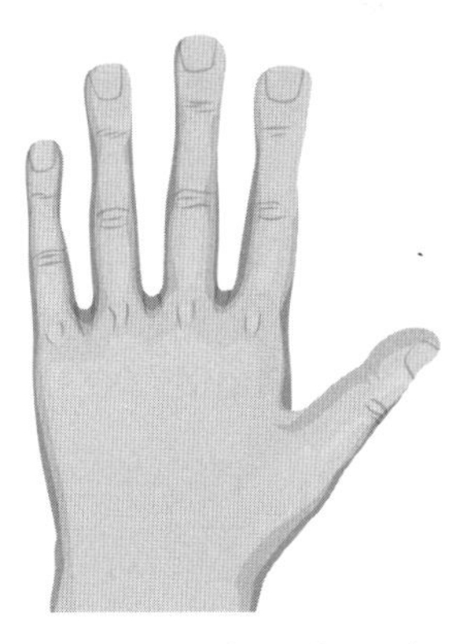

The spatulate hand

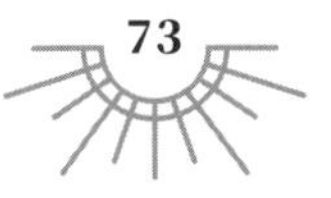

4. The philosophical hand

These long, bony hands often belong to teachers, philosophers and intellectuals who are always seeking the truth. The minutiae of life is of little concern to people with Philosophical Hands—they are far too easily distracted.

These are people who see the big picture, often ignoring their immediate surroundings to the point that their untidiness borders on the eccentric.

5. The mixed hand

Neither one thing nor the other, this is probably the most difficult to interpret. Sometimes such a hand is clawed, something that indicates long-term anxiety over financial matters, or that the person is over-timid and cautious in everything he or she does.

6. The physic or pointed hand

Graceful and conic in shape with pointed, tapering fingers and a long palm, the Physic Hand suggests an intuitive person who is happy to follow his or her own instincts and is usually quite right to do so.

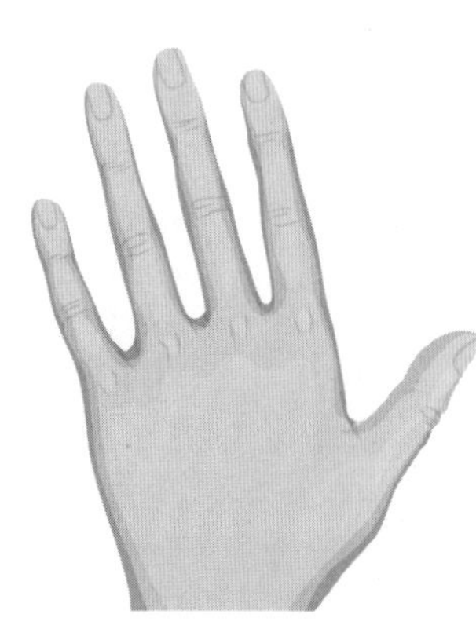

The mixed hand

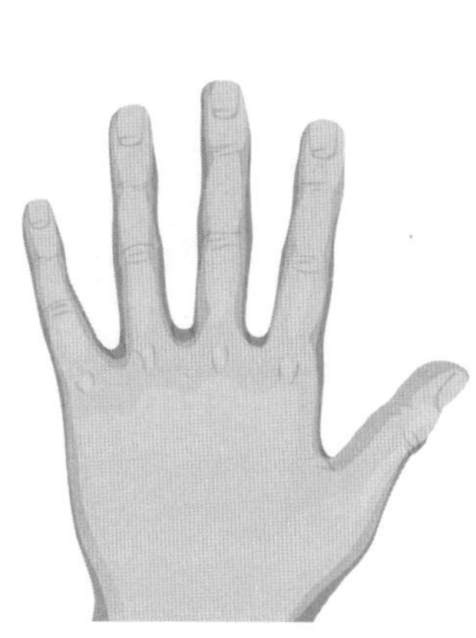

The philosophical hand

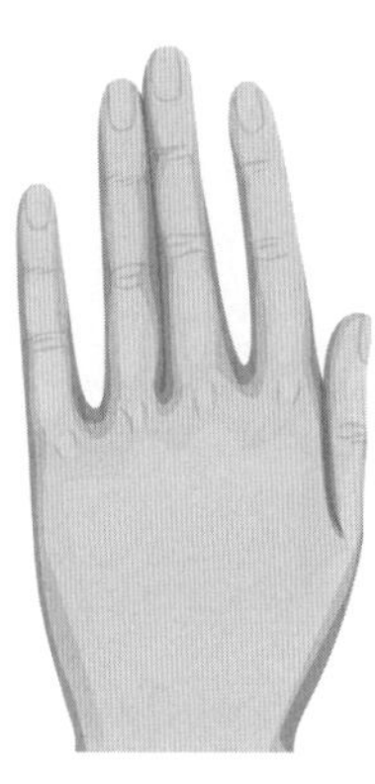

The physic or pointed hand

All Fingers and Thumbs

The first thing to look at is the thumb, which represents willpower, and see how it is held naturally. Insecure people tend to curl it up, defensively, within the palm. Then determine its size in proportion to the rest of the hand. When the lower knuckle of the dominant hand's thumb is placed at the bottom of the little finger, it should be about the same length as that finger.

Strong, thick thumbs say that the sitter has the capacity to deal with whatever life throws in his or her direction. Long ones indicate rational, clear thinking and leadership qualities. People with short thumbs tend to be subordinate to stronger characters, lacking the will to resist them, which often makes them unhappy. Aggressive tendencies are shown by short, stubby thumbs.

More information can be gleaned from the thumb's phalanges (the sections between the joints), which are read from the top down, the upper one representing will and the lower one logic. They should be about the same length. If the lower one is longer, then its owner is probably someone who thinks and talks a lot—too much to get down to actually doing anything! If the upper phalange is longer, beware a person who rushes headfirst into things and then cries for help as soon as trouble threatens.

Low self-esteem is indicated by a flattened thumb pad and is something that often manifests itself in sexual promiscuity. A square tip indicates a practical nature, while a spatulate one shows that the owner is especially good with his or her hands.

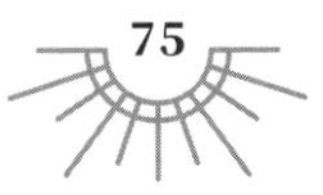

The angle of the thumb to the index finger also yields significant information. If it is less than 45° the owner has a tendency to be something of a control freak. An angle of 90° between the two says that the person is a charming extrovert, outgoing and great company. Beware a thumb that curves significantly backward; it sits in the hand of a killer—in every sense of the word.

The fingers are named as follows: the first (index) finger, Jupiter, indicates ambition and expansion. The second finger, Saturn, is connected with judgment and knowledge. The third (ring) talks of exploits and achievements; it is the finger of Apollo. And the little finger, Mercury, has to do with observation and perception.

Generally, long fingers indicate that the person is something of a perfectionist, and extra-long ones say that he or she is prone to exaggeration. Short fingers can indicate an impatient nature.

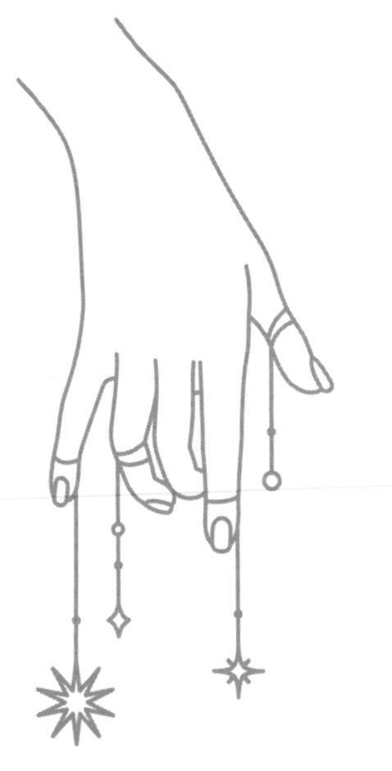

THE JUPITER FINGER

A long index finger points to self-confidence and awareness. Its owner is ambitious and more than capable of achieving these ambitions. A leader, this is a person to whom one can turn during any type of crisis. A medium-length one shows that its owner is confident when confidence is called for, and modest when humility is the order of the day. And whoever has a short index finger is shy, scared of failure, insecure, and full of self-doubt.

THE MIDDLE FINGER

A long middle finger talks of ambition without humor. Those with long middle fingers work hard to get ahead, and will surely do so. A medium-length one indicates that the owner has the maturity to know when it is time to work and when it is time to play. A short middle finger is a sign of a careless person who hates routine so much that "disorganization" is a word often used in reference to him or her.

THE RING FINGER

Often associated with creativity, a long ring finger points to an artistic nature that can lead its owner to consider design, especially fashion design, as a career. It can also warn of a gambling streak. One of medium length still points to having a creative nature, but a more traditional, conservative one. A short ring finger means that there is little creativity in its owner's nature.

THE LITTLE FINGER

Length here indicates intelligence and excellent communication skills that make their owners excellent writers and speakers. They might also have a stronger-than-average sex drive. A little finger that is medium in length says that the owner is of average intelligence—not too bright, but not particularly dim either. And a short one means emotional immaturity and a tendency toward gullibility and naïveté.

LENGTH

The comparative length of the fingers is also indicative of a person's nature. When the first finger is longer than the ring finger, this is indicative of someone who is driven by their ego. Religious leaders and senior officers in the military often have such fingers.

Where the second finger is flanked by index and ring fingers of equal length, the owner has a serious, controlled nature with a well-developed sense of curiosity.

If the third finger is longer than the index finger, then an emotional, intuitive nature is indicated, someone who makes a good doctor or nurse and whose advice is always well worth listening to.

And if the little finger rises above the top joint of the ring finger, then this is a charismatic person with a quick wit and shrewd business abilities.

SHAPE

The shapes of the fingers are also significant. Square ones show a rational, methodical nature, someone who thinks a lot at the expense of creativity. Fingers that are pointed indicate a sensitive nature, fragile daydreamers who are often artists or writers. Someone with conical fingers is usually a person with a flexible nature who often has excellent negotiating skills and to whom emotional security is important, often overly important, to their well-being.

People with spatulate fingers can be exhaustingly active, not just physically but intellectually. They are innovators and inventors, explorers and extroverts.

FINGERNAILS

Fingernails, too, play their part in hand-reading. Square ones indicate an easy-going temperament, while broad ones say, "Beware! I'm a strong character with an explosive temper!" Fan-shaped fingernails are a sign that the owner has been under stress for quite a long time. A gentle, kind nature is indicated by almond- shaped fingernails, but they can indicate that the person is prone to daydreaming. A selfish, cold personality is shown by narrow nails. Wedge-shaped nails say that the person is oversensitive and as touchy as a nervous cat.

The nails can also indicate health problems. If they are dished, then the person's chemical balance is out of kilter. Dietary deficiencies may result in horizontal ridges forming in the nails, whereas rheumatism may cause vertical ones running down the nails.

THE PHALANGES

The sections between the joints are read from the top down. The top one is concerned with introspection, the second corresponds to the subject's attitude to material concerns, and the third with physical desires.

The Major Lines of the Palm

The lines that crisscross the palms are just one of the things that professional palm-readers look at, whereas to the amateurs (and no disrespect to them) who do readings at the county fair, lines are often the only things that are considered. The professional interprets their meaning in conjunction with what we have looked at already, as well as other marks that we'll mention later.

Plotting the chronology of the subject's life, and assessing whether events have already happened or when they might happen, involves knowing where the lines begin. Horizontal lines should always be read from the thumb side of the hand, and vertical ones from the wrist. Flexibility is the keyword. Remember that in palmistry, as in all things concerned with divination, nothing is written in stone.

It is impossible to be precise as to where a line starts and where it stops. Lines differ from hand to hand. Some may be stronger in one subject than in another; some may be straight or straighter while others have pronounced curves; some will start at the wrist, others up from it. The line of one hand may stop at one particular mound while the same line on another subject's hand runs through it.

THE LIFE LINE

This is the line that curves downward, from close to the thumb toward the wrist. The closer to the thumb it starts, the less vitality the subject is likely to have, whereas the wider the curve the greater the energy. A life line that is less well defined than the head line (see below) points to a person who is driven mentally rather than physically. Chains in the life line are an indication of delicate health, and small lines rising from it denote versatility and physical activity. Lines that seem to swing out of the main one point to a desire to travel and see the world.

Upward hooks along the line, after some unfortunate event has been indicated in the reading, suggest that the sitter has made a tremendous effort to get back on his or her feet after a setback; otherwise they indicate achievement.

Splits along the line point to huge change or conflict—perhaps between domestic and professional life, or in a new job or relationship.

THE HEART LINE

This is the topmost major line, running horizontally from the side of the hand opposite the thumb. It's the line that reveals relationships, not just romantic ones. If it is almost straight, romance plays little part in the subject's life: he or she views other people in a chilly, rational way. A strongly curved heart line points to the subject who loves being in love and shows it, the sort of person who takes the lead in any relationship.

A heart line that curves steeply below the index and middle digits indicates strong sexual desires and passions—not promiscuity, though. That can be shown by a short heart line close to the finger and points to the mound of Saturn (see below). Such a line also denotes

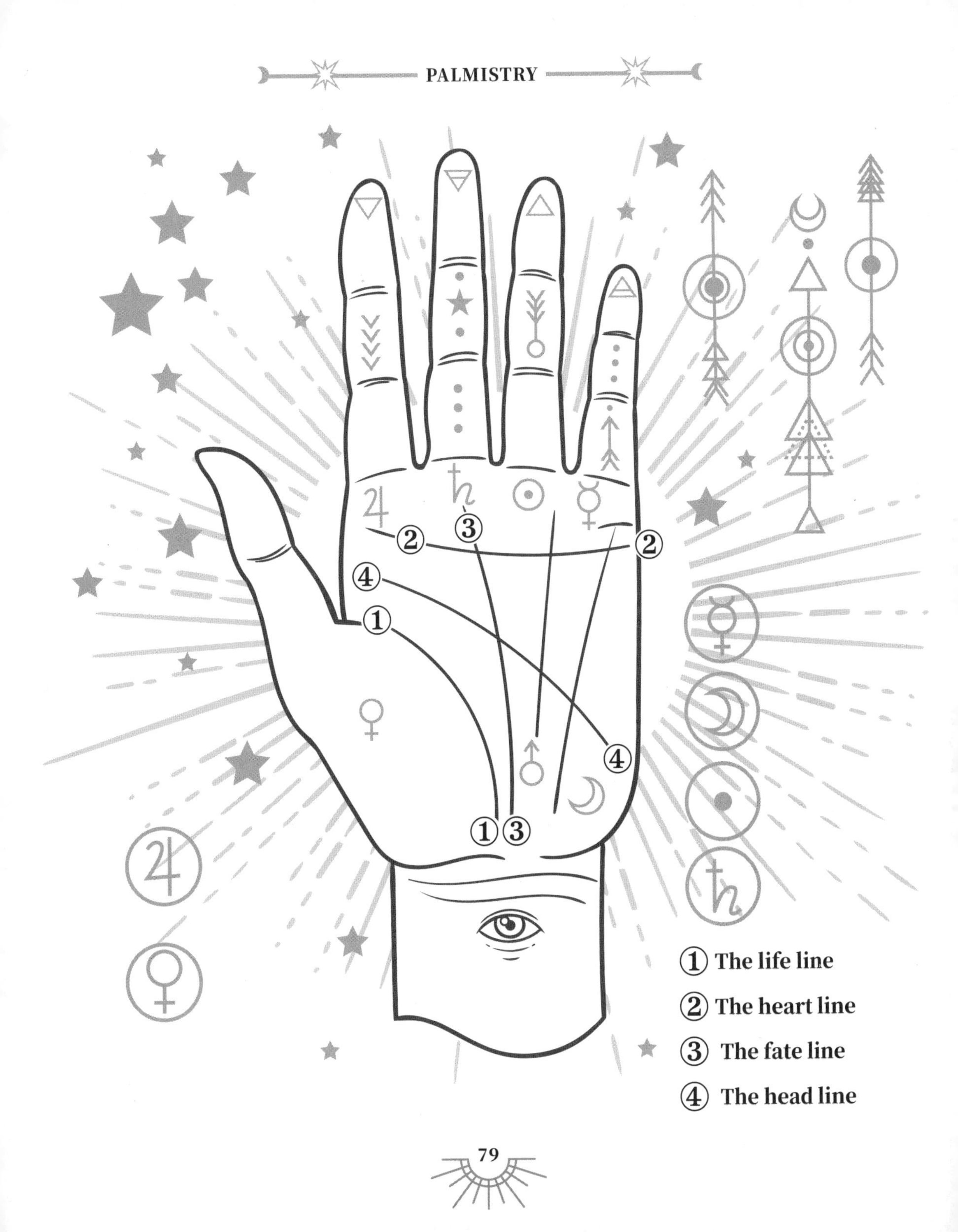
① The life line
② The heart line
③ The fate line
④ The head line

practicality in matters of the heart. But a line that ends under the middle finger says that the subject is the sort of person who is in constant need of love and reassurance.

If there are lots of branches off the heart line, the sitter enjoys meeting new people and establishing friendships with them.

THE FATE LINE

The line that runs from the wrist and runs upward toward the mound of Saturn represents career, marriage, and children—the practical, central supporting aspects of life. A strong fate line indicates that the subject has settled into life's routines and accepts them happily. If it is not there, or is very faint, then the sitter is unsettled and might have to change jobs several times before they make their way in life, and will have to do so with little or no help from their family. But one that begins in the mound of Venus (see below) suggests that the family will interfere, particularly in romantic matters and those relating to the sitter achieving his or her ambitions.

A fate line that almost reaches the middle finger says that the subject will enjoy an active old age. One that begins at the head line suggests that academic effort has played an important part in the subject achieving success in life. One that stops at the heart line is an indication of sexual indiscretion.

An overly thick fate line means a period of anxiety at the time of life indicated by the chronology of the reading.

THE HEAD LINE

The head line runs between the life and heart lines. If it starts off tied to the life line at the start, slavish obedience to and dependence on other people is indicated. If the two lines have distinct starting points (which is usual), a well-balanced, independent nature is indicated.

A long head line points to a person who thinks before they act; a short one to someone who is quick-thinking and incisive. If the line doesn't slant at all, the subject is likely to be an unsympathetic person lacking in imagination. A slanting line indicates an imaginative and intuitive person. A line that curves rather than slants indicates lateral thinking.

Receptivity to new people is shown by the presence of lots of outward branches on the head line. If they point toward the mound of Jupiter (see below), leadership qualities are suggested. If they point to Saturn, a hardworking nature is indicated as well as success in a job that requires research. Artistic achievement is indicated by branches that point toward Apollo, and someone with branches pointing toward the mound of Mercury should look to a career in the communications industry or business world. Downward branches suggest periods of depression, but one that runs to the lunar mound opposite the thumb can expect success in the arts or humanities.

THE TRIANGLE AND THE QUADRANT

The triangular shape that is often formed by the head, heart, and life lines also has a meaning, as does the area between the heart and head lines, which is known as the quadrant.

A wide triangle is an indication of an open person, always willing to take action and with passions that are easily aroused. Meanness of spirit is indicated by a small, cramped triangle.

A wide quadrant is an indication of an impulsive nature that cares little about what the world thinks. But a small quadrant marked with many lines suggests timidity and fear, someone who is constantly concerned about what people think of them.

THE MINOR LINES

Whereas most of us have the major lines engraved in the palms of our hands, many of us will not have all of the lines that follow—and their absence can be as significant as their presence.

The success line

Often called the Line of Apollo, the line that runs vertically from the palm toward the ring finger is the line of fame, fortune, and success in that which the subject finds important. If it is not there, the subject believes that success can only come through hard work. If there is a break in it, a period of some kind of struggle is indicated.

The health line

Ideally, the line that on many hands runs up the radial side of the hand, toward the little finger, and which is sometimes called the Line of Mercury, should not be present, because it indicates an overdeveloped concern for health. One that starts close to the mound of Venus (see below) suggests bad digestion, and a long health line on a very lined hand says that worry could cause ulcers.

The Mars line

Running inside the life line, this is an indication of someone who has vitality with a capital V.

The via lascivia

A horizontal line that runs across the mound of the Moon (see below) can indicate that the subject suffers from allergies or that an addiction is causing problems.

The girdle of Venus

If it is present at all, seen as a semicircle above the heart line and covering the mounds of Saturn and Apollo (see below), it says that the subject is a person of an unusually sensitive nature.

Travel lines

Running horizontally from the outer side of the hand below the little finger, and lying across the mound of the Moon (see below) in the lower left corner and on the lower Mars mound (see below), these little lines indicate important journeys. And the stronger and longer they are, the more important the journey is.

Bracelets

These are the horizontal lines between the wrist and the palm. Three of them indicate a long life. If the top one curves and pushes up towards the palm, it could mean that infertility is a problem.

The bow of intuition

A very unusual line found opposite the thumb, starting at the mound of the Moon (see below) and curving up toward the mound of Mercury (see below), this is an indication of intuition and prophetic ability.

The ring of Saturn

Another rare line, seen as a small arc below the middle finger, this indicates a reclusive nature and miserly tendencies.

The ring of Solomon

People who are respected for their common sense often have this line, which runs around the base of the index finger, skirting the mound of Jupiter (see below).

THE MOUNDS

The raised pads on the hands are called "mounds" or "mounts," and vary in size and the degree to which they are pronounced. They speak of the subject's character. Running widdershins from the base of the thumb, the mounds are as follows:

The mound of Venus

Found at the base of the thumb, the mound of Venus has to do with harmony and love. Broad and well-developed, it suggests a strong sex life and a love of all that is sensual, but also a deep love of the family. Sitting high and soft to the touch, it is an indication of excitability and fickleness. If it is depressed or flat, then the subject may be indolent and careless—but this could also be caused by ill health.

The mound of Neptune

Sitting at the base of the palm, in the middle of the hand, the mound of Neptune is often not prominent, but when it is, and is well developed, then the subject is probably a person of some charisma.

The mound of the Moon

At the bottom of the ulna side of the hand, the mound of the Moon is related to travel and to the unconscious. If it is very pronounced, it suggests a person of vivid imagination but an introspective nature, with a tendency to mendacity.

Sensitivity and a perceptive nature are indicated by a normal-sized Moon mound, while those who have a flat one are probably dull, unimaginative, and unstable people with a frosty nature.

Mars lower

Found on the outside edge of the hand above the mound of the Moon, this represents motivation. If it is large, though, there is a tendency toward violence and argument, while a small one may say that the subject is something of a coward. A normal Mars lower suggests courage, someone who will pick up the gauntlet and fight for a cause he or she believes in.

The mound of Mercury

Positioned at the base of the little finger, this is the mound of self-expression, travel, and business abilities. A large one suggests a good sense of humor and a warm, receptive nature. Powers of persuasion, subtlety, and quick thinking are indicated by a normal-size one. But if it is flat, the subject could be a bit of a dull loner, shy perhaps, or just lazy.

The mound of Apollo or the Sun

Situated at the base of the ring finger, this mound has to do with success, charm, and creativity. High achievers in the media, on stage, and in sports often have pronounced mounds of Apollo, but they can be prone to hedonism, extravagance, and pretentiousness. An undeveloped one indicates a person who is dull, whose life is aimless, and who has no interest in culture whatsoever.

The mound of Saturn

Sitting at the base of the middle finger, this mound, if over-prominent, suggests someone who is gloomy bordering on reclusive, and intent on keeping his or her head down and earning money. If it is flat or undeveloped, he or she is your ordinary person in the street. If the mound merges with Jupiter (see below), it implies someone who is ambitious and serious. And if it merges with the mound of Apollo (see above), then the subject could be passionate about the arts.

The mound of Jupiter

This mound sits at the base of the index finger. Representing how willpower can be used to achieve ambition, the mound of Jupiter, if well-rounded, suggests that its owner is confident that he or she will succeed. People with large Jupiters like everything to be just so, but they can be generous. If the mound is especially high, then arrogance is a word that is probably associated with the subject. A flat, undeveloped Jupiter is a sign of laziness, selfishness, and a dislike of authority.

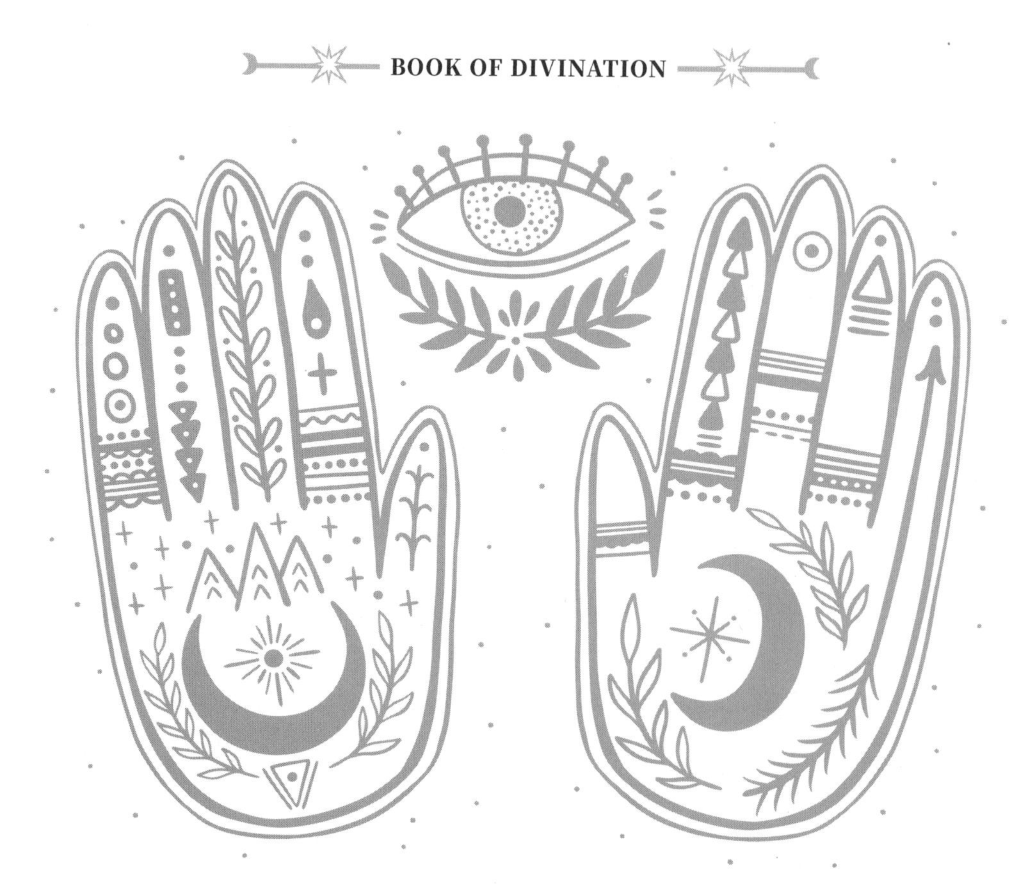

Mars upper

In the crease of the thumb, a large Mars upper is a sign of bad temper and cruelty, and a sharp, sarcastic tongue. Moral courage is indicated by a normal Mars upper, and cowardliness by a flat one.

The plain of Mars

Not a mound, obviously, the plain of Mars is in the hollow in the center of the palm. If the lines around it are distinct and unbroken, the subject probably enjoys good health and prosperity, and can look forward to a long life. Optimism is indicated by a flat plain, but if it is hollow, then in all likelihood the subject lacks both drive and ambition.

Minor marks

As well as using the lines and mounds, diviners can get information from the small marks that many of us carry in the palms of our hands.

Ascending lines

Branching upwards from the main lines of the hand, these indicate extra energy, and if they continue onward, toward one of the mounds, that mound indicates the realm in which that energy is directed.

Crosses

Crosses are not a good sign, because they draw out negative aspects of the line on which they are found, although the less distinct the cross

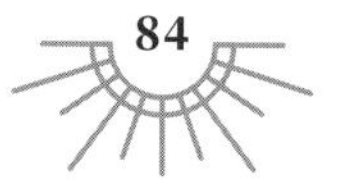

is, the less powerful the draw will be. A cross on the mound of Apollo indicates business or financial disappointment, whereas one on the mound of Mercury signifies a dishonest personality.

Relationships will suffer if there is a cross on Venus. A cross on the mound of the Moon suggests someone prone to self-delusion. But worst of all is a cross on the mound of Saturn, because it signifies that ambitions will be particularly hard to achieve.

Descending lines

Just as an ascending line indicates an energy surge, descending ones point to there being less energy directed toward the areas governed by the line from which they fork.

Forked lines

On any of the major lines, forks indicate diversity related to that particular line. Forks on the life line may mean a change in direction at the time indicated by where the fork is. Love affairs or perhaps a change in where the affections lie can be suggested by forks in the heart line. A fork at the end of the fate line points to a successful career bringing fame and fortune. And a fork at the end of the head line is a sign that the subject is a good businessperson.

Grilles

Often found on the mounts of the hand, these little checkerboards denote obstacles ahead in whatever the mound is associated with. Thus, a grille on Venus suggests greedy lust.

Islands

Uneven circles on lines and mounds indicate weakness, listlessness, and unwelcome change, but changes that could lead to better things—eventually. On the life line, for example, islands close to the start mean troubled teenage years. On the heart line, they can signify problems with hearing or sight.

Stars

Something spectacular is in the air when there are stars on the mounds of the hand. On Jupiter (at the base of the index finger), it indicates a good marriage that will enhance career prospects with a consequent boost to finances. On Saturn (base of the middle finger), it suggests that the subject's special talents will bring fame and fortune. On Apollo (base of the ring finger), a star might indicate a major win or an artistic triumph, whereas a great step forward in knowledge is indicated by a star on Mercury (base of the little finger).

7

Runes

The word "rune" means secret writing. Casting the runes—stones on which mystic symbols are engraved—began several thousand years ago in Scandinavia, and has its roots in Scandinavian mythology. The symbols represent animals and other things from the natural world, although their precise meanings are lost to us.

Runes were dedicated to Odin, the supreme deity in the Scandinavian pantheon, and associated with travel, healing, communication, wisdom, and divination. According to Scandinavian myth, in his search for enlightenment, Odin hung himself upside down on Yggdrasil, the World Tree, and impaled himself on his own spear for nine days.

On the ground, rune stones hidden in Yggdrasil's roots revealed themselves.

The legend probably has its own roots in the mythology of the Volsungr, a tribe of priest-magicians and guardians of the ancient forests, who used an early form of runes (Ur Runes) to divine the future. At the end of the last Ice Age, the Volsungr spread south, bringing their knowledge with them. Later, they retreated back whence they came, but by then runic divination had already spread throughout Scandinavia and into central Europe.

By Roman times, the runes had evolved into Futhark, a runic alphabet. Interpreting the meaning of the stones was a mystery granted only to a few. The Roman historian Tacitus, writing in *Germania*, described a runic ceremony during which a branch was cut from a nut-bearing tree and cut into small pieces (rune slips) on which runic symbols were marked. These were cast on a white cloth and interpreted by a priest.

Whenever a journey had to be made, the runes were cast to establish the most propitious time to set out. So the runes followed the trade routes across Europe and into Mediterranean lands. The Vikings took them from their homeland to America, Russia, Turkey, Greece, and

even as far as North Africa, as evidenced by the runic carvings found on monuments and other artifacts in these parts of the world.

In Anglo-Saxon England, kings and bishops had the power to read the runes, but the practice gradually died out, not just in Britain but in other parts of the world where Christianity (which regarded the use of runes as Pagan) was taking hold. Some people continued to cast them, and some people continued to believe what they said, but just as those who read the future through other means often came to be regarded as harmless eccentrics at best, dangerous heretics at worst, casting the runes was sidelined as something of a "party trick."

Interest in them was renewed during the rise of German nationalism in the nineteenth and twentieth centuries, when there was a revival of interest in Teutonic folklore, fueled in no small part by Wagnerian opera. However, when this revival came to be intricately linked with Nazism, the runes once again fell into disfavor.

But with the revival of the New Age movement, runes have again become popular, not just for divining the future and increasing one's knowledge of oneself, but to be carried as talismans, each sign having its own association.

The runes that are popularly used today are the Germanic Futhark set, which is divided into three sets ("aettirs") of eight runes each, making twenty-four in all. Each of these aettirs is named after a Norse deity. The first eight are dedicated to Freya, the goddess of love and lust, war and death; Hagal, the guardian of the other gods and goddesses in the Norse pantheon, presides over the second set; and Tiwaz, god of justice and law, of war, and of the sky, rules the third aettir.

The qualities of these three gods influence the runes in the aettir dedicated to them, each rune having a double meaning—a material one and a spiritual one. Nine of them read the same whichever way they are looked at. The others can be drawn upright or reversed. But any of the runes may appear as a "merkstave" (which literally means "dark stick" and implies a "dark" meaning), depending on how they are cast. Note that a "reversed" or "merkstave" meaning is not the opposite of its primary meaning, but usually has a more negative connotation.

Runes can help you look deeply into the inner self, pinpointing fears and desires and highlighting the hidden factors that will shape the future. They describe positive and negative influences, pointing out ways to use the former and overcome the latter, and to make constructive choices for the future.

The way in which the runes can be interpreted is given below. Being of such antiquity, there are variations in the names of each. We give the two most commonly used names for each symbol along with the literal runic meaning and the facet of life with which it is most intimately associated.

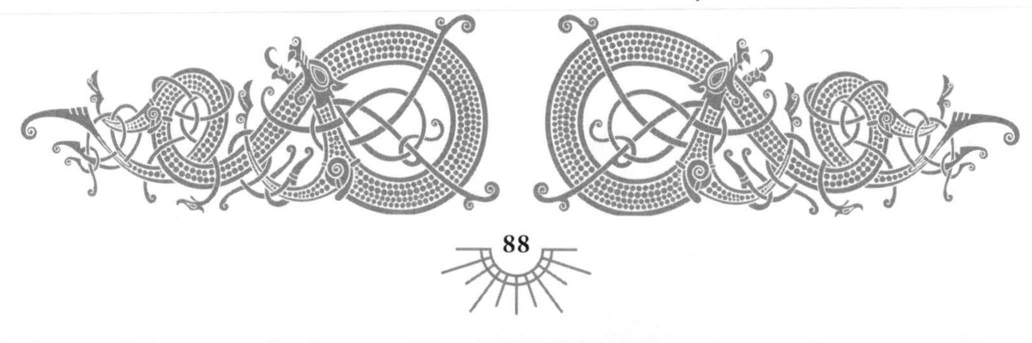

Freya's Aettir

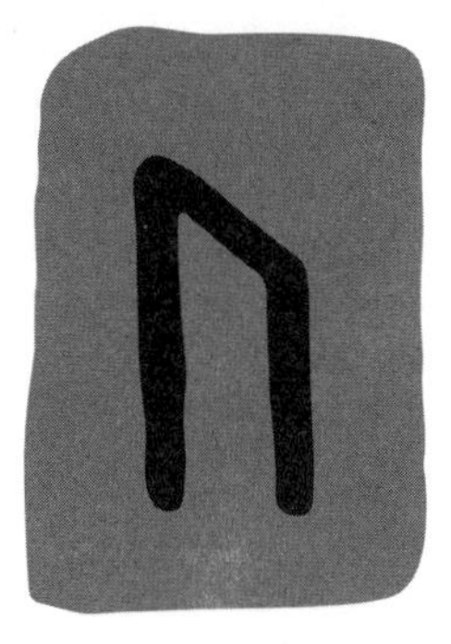

FEHU/FEOH
(Cattle = possessions and prosperity)

This is a sign of prosperity and material gain, probably from past efforts being rewarded. It signifies foresight and fertility and, as an energetic rune, it speaks of new opportunities and social success. Reversed or merkstave, it signifies that what has been achieved—either tangible or intangible, such as self-esteem—may be lost. It also indicates failure, perhaps brought about by greed or stupidity. As a talisman, Fehu is good for achieving a goal, gaining a promotion, or bringing luck to a new business.

URUZ/UR
(Bison = strength)

A rune of strength, courage, and overcoming obstacles, the right way up it can indicate that what seemed to have been a loss is in fact an opportunity in disguise. It speaks of action and good health, and promises wisdom and the chance to gain a deeper insight into oneself. Reversed or merkstave, it suggests a character that is too easily led or influenced by others, something that can lead the subject into the land of lost opportunity. Drawn this way, it also threatens ill health, inconsistency, ignorance, callousness, brutality, and violence. Anyone seeking a surge in sexual potency or a stronger will should wear Ur as a talisman.

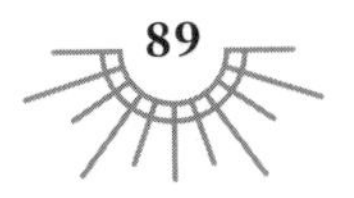

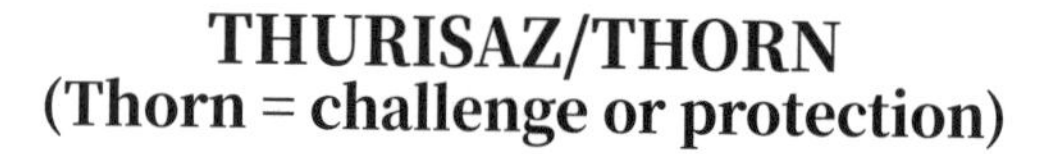

THURISAZ/THORN
(Thorn = challenge or protection)

Drawn or falling the right way up, Thurisaz suggests change of some kind and is also concerned with male sexuality and fertility. It can indicate the approach of a destructive force or conflict, but one that will be driven away if instincts are listened to and followed. Merkstave or reversed, Thurisaz warns of vulnerability leading to some kind of danger. It whispers of betrayal and its approach, perhaps in the form of a malicious person with evil in their heart. Wear this rune as a talisman if seeking help in study or meditation, or the resolution of an unfortunate situation.

ANSUZ/OSS
(A god = communication)

An increased awareness of what the future holds is heralded when Ansuz appears. With its direct association with Odin, this is a rune of inspiration, wisdom, aspirations, and communication. It promises spiritual renewal and progress, clear vision, and good health. Appearing the wrong way, Ansuz implies that manipulative, selfish people will bring misunderstanding in their wake, which will lead to a feeling of disillusionment. It also warns to be on guard lest vanity and pomposity rear their ugly heads to the detriment of the subject. As a talisman, it helps in divination and in making wise decisions. It is also useful if the wearer seeks leadership.

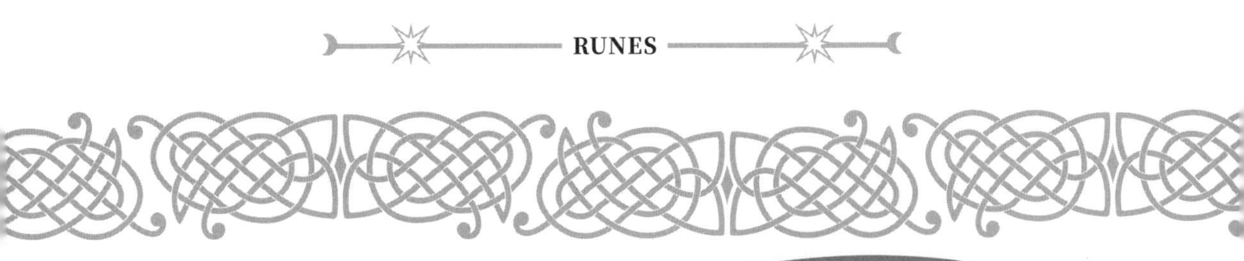

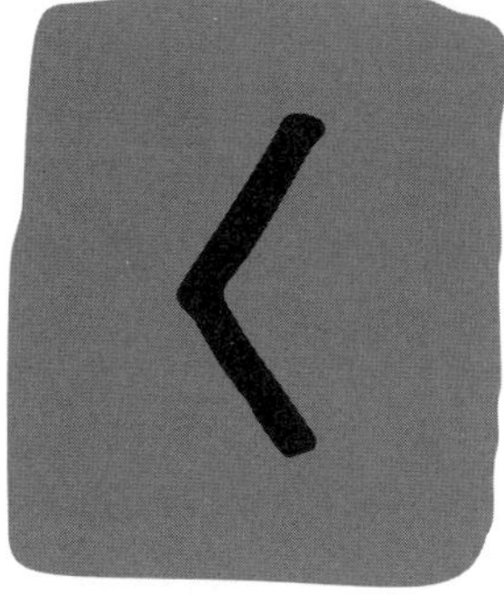

RAIDO/RIT
(Riding = action)

An indication of travel in its many guises, be it physical (such as a vacation), a change of location, a change of lifestyle, or perhaps a spiritual journey as the soul moves towards its destiny. It offers the chance to put things in perspective. Drawn merkstave or reversed, Raido suggests that a crisis of some kind is brewing or that injustice and irrationality will threaten disruption, bringing delusion in its wake. It can also suggest that the querent feels caged in by present circumstances. As a talisman, it protects travelers, brings change, and eases unfortunate situations, particularly if a reconnection of some kind is being looked for.

KANO/KENAZ/KAON
(Torch = inner wisdom)

This is a rune of the inner voice and inner strength, of guidance and illumination. It promises that light will be cast into the dark places, bringing regeneration in its glow. It promises the ability to create new realities that bring with them hope and invigorating strength. Face down or reversed, though, it stifles creativity and says that illness and negative influences—dissolution, hopelessness, mendacity, and despair—will cloud life in the immediate future. Wear or carry a Kenaz rune as a talisman to dispel anxiety and fear, for inspiration and creativity.

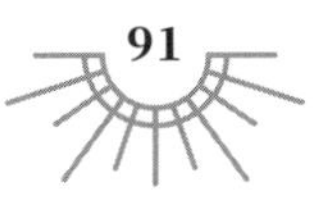

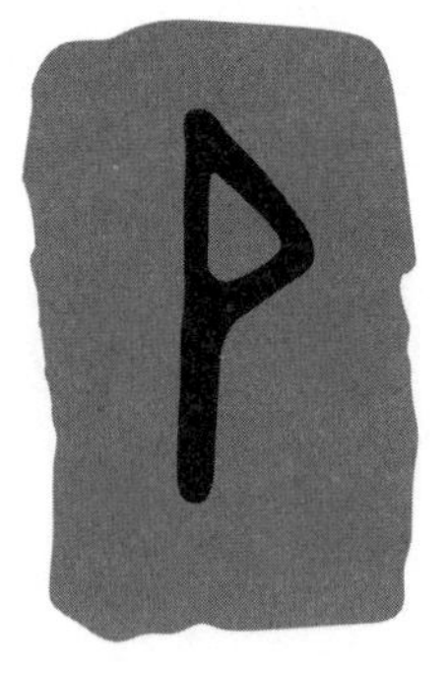

GEBO/GIFU
(Gift = partnership)

Generosity is a word that is often associated with Gebo, which relates to all kinds of exchanges including contracts, love, marriage, and sexual congress. Gebo promises balance and equality. It is a rune that cannot appear reversed, but if it is cast merkstave, then greed and loneliness will cast their shadows, causing spiritual and emotional emptiness. Gebo is an excellent talisman to strengthen a relationship and to bring luck and fertility.

WUNJO/WUNNA
(Joy = pleasure)

Bringing comfort, joy, and pleasure in its wake, along with the promise of prosperity, good fellowship, and harmony, Wunjo also warns of the dangers of going to extremes. But if a little self-control is exercised, the querent will benefit from their true worth being recognized. When it appears the wrong way, Wunjo warns of sorrow and strife, and of being alienated. It whispers of delays, of the dangers of drinking too much, and of being possessed by uncontrollable rages. Worn as a talisman, Wunjo helps to motivate, and to bring unfinished tasks to successful conclusions.

Hagal's Aettir

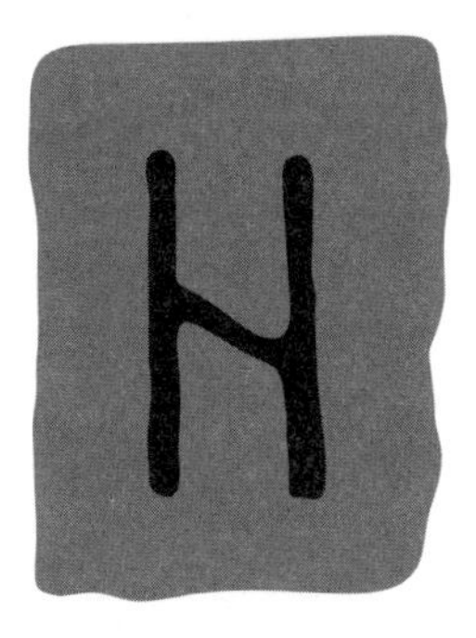

HAGALAZ/HAGAL
(Chaos = change and destruction)

Hagalaz, the Mother Rune, indicates uncontrolled forces wreaking havoc, disrupting plans, and ushering in a time of trials and tests. But all is not lost, because Hagal also suggests that the crises will lead to completion or closure of some kind that heralds an inner harmony. Merkstave (it cannot be reversed), it says that a catastrophic natural disaster may be about to strike. And on a personal level, it indicates a loss of power and a period of stagnation, hardship, and loss, perhaps brought about by ill health. As a talisman, Hagalaz removes unwanted influences and what appears to be a circle of never-ending destruction.

NAUDHIZ/NAUT/NYD
(Need = constraint)

Representing needs that can be met by reacting positively to deprivation, Naudhiz says that conflict can be overcome by willpower, that delays and restriction can be endured (and have to be), and that fears have to be faced. Reversed or merkstave, it suggests that freedom will be restricted and that self-control is essential as poverty and deprivation beckon. It also hints at emotional hunger. Wear it as a talisman if there is a need that has to be fulfilled, or to turn a negative fate into a positive one.

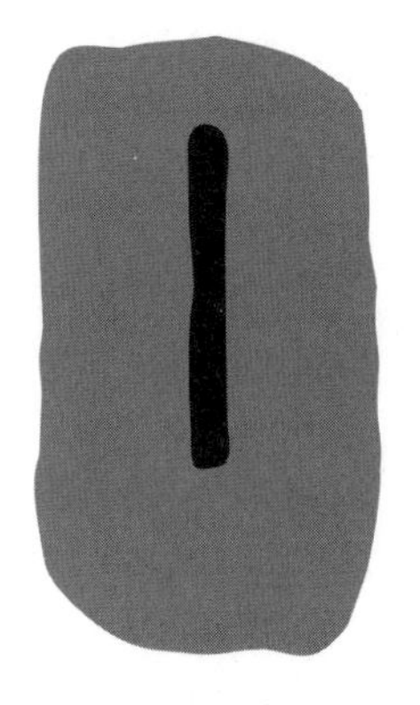

ISA/IS
(Ice = standstill or stillness)

Another rune that is irreversible, this is a reinforcing rune, underlining the message of those around it. It talks of challenging frustrations, that creativity is being blocked by psychological forces, and that this time of standstill is a time to look inward and wait for clarity to appear. Merkstave it is a ghastly rune, presaging treachery and deceit, and warning the querent to beware of being ambushed by the plotting of others. As a talisman, it can be worn to give breathing space or to bring something to an end.

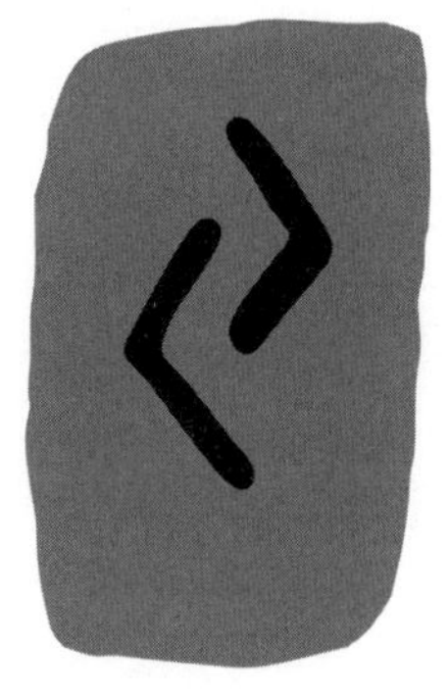

JERA/YER
(Year = harvest and life cycles)

This is the rune of the harvest, when the results of previous efforts can be gathered. It heralds a happy period of peace. Jera also says that a breakthrough of some type will bring a period when things have become stagnant. Merkstave (Jera can't be reversed), it warns of an unexpected reversal of fortune, which may mean a major change in life. Conflict becomes unavoidable, poverty beckons, and timing goes awry. Wear it as a talisman to encourage change and fertility.

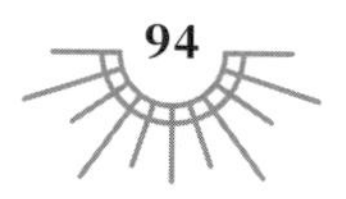

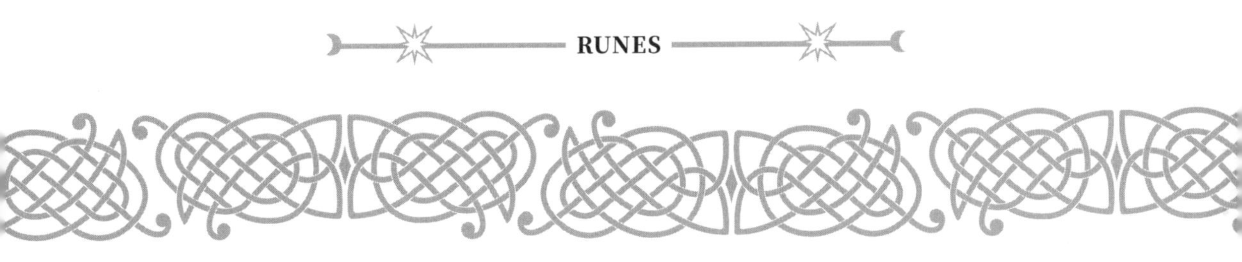

EIWAZ/YR
(Yew = endings and mysteries)

The yew tree represents the cycle of death and rebirth, and when Eiwaz appears, it suggests natural endings leading to new beginnings. Changes and turning points, maybe brought about by fears being confronted, lie around the corner. Merkstave, it warns of confusion and destruction, and an inability to get around something that is blocking the way. As a talisman, it can bring about huge changes or show the way around huge difficulties.

PERTHRO/PEORTH
(Dice cup = initiation, the essence of one's being)

A rune that indicates that deep transformative powers are at work, this is the rune of what has yet to be revealed, and of taking chances. It can indicate mystery, secrecy, and psychic abilities. Merkstave, it warns of harmful addiction and stagnation, bringing with it an inability to understand others and a sense of finality. As a talisman, it helps divination and enhances psychic powers. Pregnant women often wear or carry Perthro, as it is believed to ease the pain of childbirth.

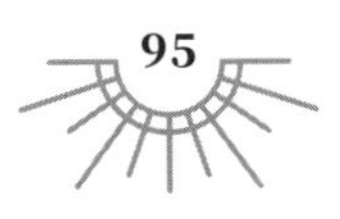

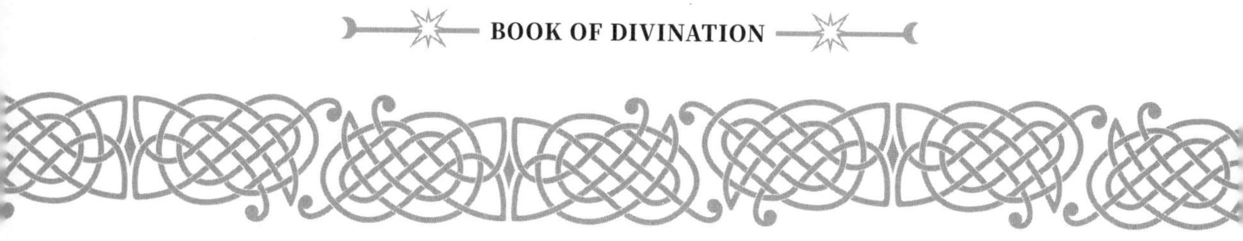

ALGIZ/AQUIZI
(Elk-sledge = protection)

This is often regarded as one of the most difficult runes to interpret. It suggests that help will come from an unexpected quarter to ward off a threat of some kind. Algiz also offers a connection to the powers in whose hands our fate lies, and encourages us to channel our energies toward the greater good. Reversed, it is a sign that hidden dangers lie ahead, ill health may be about to strike, and a warning to consider any advice from a third party before acting on it. Algiz protects as a talisman and helps build defenses.

SOWILO/SIG
(Sun = wholeness and potential)

The rune of potential and success, energy and expansion, Sowilo promises that goals will be achieved and honor bestowed. It presages a union between the conscious and the unconscious, but it also counsels restraint. Merkstave, it speaks of bad advice leading to false goals being set, of despair, and of retribution. Sowilo, as a talisman, gives a boost to energy levels, increases strength, and generally encourages enthusiasm.

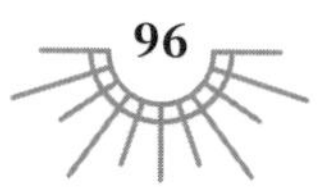

Tiwaz's Aettir

TIWAZ/TIU
(Star = justice and victory)

Honor, justice, leadership, and authority are words commonly associated with Tiwaz. The rune says that the questioner knows where his true strengths lie and points to a willingness to self-sacrifice. It predicts victory and success in a competition that is on the horizon, or in a legal matter in which the subject is involved. Reversed or merkstave, it suggests a reversal in energies and creative flow. It hints that the querent suffers from mental stagnation, that he or she is over-analytical and prone to self-sacrifice. As a talisman, Tiwaz protects material surroundings, brings victory, strengthens will, and can help heal wounds.

BERKANO/BIRCA
(Birch = rebirth)

Berkano is the rune of birth, general fertility, mental, physical and personal growth, and liberation. Berkano brings the light of spring with it, promising new growth and new beginnings. A meeting might be heralded that will bring with it arousal and desire. Berkano also promises that an enterprise or new venture that has already begun will be successful and bring prosperity. Reversed or merkstave, it is a warning of family problems and domestic troubles, and that someone close to the querent is causing anxiety. If this rune is cast the wrong way, beware carelessness and loss of control, a blurred consciousness, deceit, sterility, and stagnation. As a talisman, Berkano can be used to heal infections, bring about a good harvest, and make a fresh start.

EHWAZ/EH
(Horse = harmony)

Transportation—a horse, car, plane, boat, or any other means—is indicated when Ehwaz appears. It heralds change, and change for the better, brought about by gradual development and steady progress. The rune promises harmony and teamwork, trust and loyalty. If a marriage is in the works when Ehwaz appears, it will be an ideal one. It also confirms beyond any doubt the meaning of the runes around it in a reading. Reversed or merkstave, it is not necessarily a bad sign, but suggests a craving for change, a restlessness or confinement in a situation not of the subject's making. But it can also presage reckless haste, disharmony, mistrust, and betrayal. Wear Ehwaz as a talisman to bring power.

MANNAZ/MAN
(Man = the self, humanity, and tradition)

Mannaz talks of the subject's attitude toward others and their attitude toward the subject; it mentions friends and enemies, and social order. Mannaz is concerned with intelligence, forethought, and creative skills and abilities. When the rune appears, the querent can expect to receive some type of aid or cooperation. Reversed or merkstave, it is a warning of depression, mortality, blindness, and self-delusion. And if that wasn't bad enough, it also tells the subject to beware cunning, slyness, and manipulation, and says that no matter where help is sought, it won't be found. A Mannaz rune can be worn as a talisman to represent someone else or a group of people, and to establish social relationships.

LAGUZ/LAGU (Water = life forces and emotions)

Laguz is a rune of the sea, of water's ebb and flow, and of the healing power of renewal. It emphasizes imagination and psychic matters, dreams and fantasies, the mysteries of the unknown. It hints at the importance of what is hidden or belongs to the underworld. Reversed or merkstave, Laguz is an indication of a period of confusion in the subject's life, and that wrong decisions may be made through lack of proper judgment. As a talisman, Laguz enhances psychic abilities, and helps those who wear or carry it face up to their fears. It stabilizes emotional disorders and helps uncover what is hidden.

INGWAZ/ING (The earth god = people)

Ingwaz is concerned with male fertility, gestation, and internal growth. It is all about common sense and simple strengths, home and love of family, caring and human warmth. It presages a period of rest and relaxation, when anxieties disappear, loose ends are tied up, and querents find themselves free to move in new directions. Irreversible, if Ingwaz appears merkstave, it brings impotence, movement without change, and hard work that brings little reward. Wear Ingwaz as a talisman to bring fertility and growth or to encourage good health and restore balance.

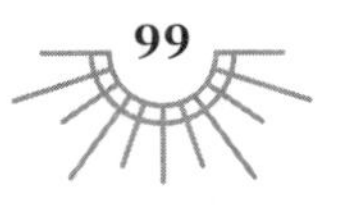

OTHALA/ODAL
(Homestead = ancestral property)

A rune of possessions, house, and home, and what the subject holds to be truly important in his or her life. It is also a rune of groups, promising order and prosperity. It is also concerned with homeland and spiritual heritage, experience, and fundamental values. It promises aid in spiritual and physical journeys. It is a source of safety and abundance. Reversed or merkstave, it forewarns of customary order and totalitarianism. It promises bad karma, prejudice, and narrow-minded provincialism. As a talisman, Othala helps the wearer acquire property, bring a project to a successful conclusion, and strengthen family ties.

DAGAZ/DAG
(Day = integration)

Dagaz suggests the dawning of breakthrough, awareness, and awakening. It promises that clarity will light up the subject's life, and says that now is the time to embark on a new enterprise. When Dagaz is drawn up, the subject is being told that using one's will can bring about desired change. It talks of security and certainty, growth and release. Merkstave (it cannot be reversed), it is not a particularly bad sign, presaging completion and ending, although at worst it can say that hope is about to be lost. As a talisman, Dagaz brings a positive outcome to any situation that concerns the carrier.

Runic Spreads

Modern rune sets often contain a blank one. Being an invention of the 1980s, there is no historical support for this and it should not be used by anyone who takes the runes seriously. But those who do use it refer to it as Wyrd and interpret it as a sign that all possibilities are open, that life is what you make it, although it does acknowledge outside influences that are beyond the subject's control. Being blank, it cannot be cast reversed or merkstave.

Traditionalists also scorn the use of rune cards—the term is hopefully self-explanatory—but they are convenient and can be slipped into a handbag or pocket more easily than a bag containing twenty-four stones. They can also be used more discreetly when a question arises suddenly and a believer wishes to consult the runes to find the answer.

Both cards and stones are readily available at specialist shops. Some people prefer to make their own, and do so with appropriate ceremony. Whatever you choose, keep the runes in a special bag (velvet or silk is best), perhaps in a color with which the user has special associations.

There are several spreads that can be used to divine the future by casting the runes. The twelve-rune circle is one that is often used, as are the nine-stone sacred grid and the cross. Many commercially available rune sets come with instructions on these and other ways of using them, which are often based on Tarot spreads.

But perhaps the simplest (and simplicity is often the most effective) is the three-rune spread, whereby the querent focuses on a question and casts three runes. The first one indicates the situation, the second the action required, and the third the outcome. Once the various symbols, their meanings, and the variations that result in a rune being drawn merkstave have been understood, it is not too difficult to use the runes to help find the answer to any question.

8

Prophetic dreaming

The knowledge that can be acquired through dreams opens up a whole library of creativity that is ours to use if we have the courage. Our biggest problem is that unless we have undergone some kind of training to remember and/or categorize our dreams, or unless we are creative and can think laterally, it is easy to forget the content of our dreams. Even when we do remember, if our thought processes tend toward the logical, we may not believe what the dream is telling us.

Most of us aren't in the position of 19th-century scientist Friedrich Kekule, who was able to prove the validity of one of his dreams with a piece of ground-breaking science. While trying to solve the structure of the benzene molecule, Kekule dreamed of a snake eating its own tail. This gave him vital information he had been searching for: that the molecules formed a complete ring. This particular symbol echoes the *ouroboros* (the symbol of the cycle of existence), which is often used in magical workings as a protective device.

Dreams can give us a much wider perspective and a new appreciation of magical and spiritual skills. One definition of spirituality is the awareness of dimensions of existence beyond that of the purely physical. It is thought that babies in the womb "dream" themselves into physical existence. Dreams also give us access to another dimension of being: spirituality and the use of power. In fact, many Eastern cultures see sleep as a preparation for death, and a learning experience to be savored.

Today, many people will admit to having creative flashes of inspiration following dreams. It is as though a missing piece of a puzzle suddenly falls into place, allowing them to see the whole picture and therefore to make sense of a creative problem. Often a fragment of music, poetry, or apparent doggerel will linger in the mind that, on consideration, is

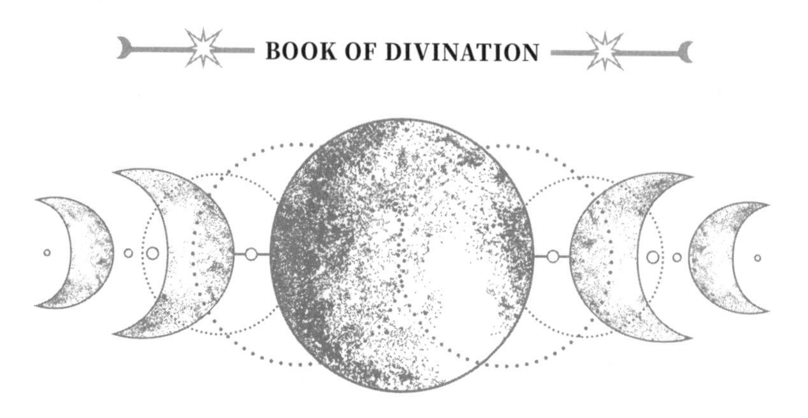

not as beautiful or pertinent as it seemed in the dream, but contains the seeds of an idea or project. The mind has opened up to possibilities and potentials far beyond the waking consciousness. Meditation can often aid in the process of creative dreaming, whether we use it to open up to the creative self before sleep or after dreaming to gain a greater understanding. As adults, with the realization that we are very much part of a greater whole, we can begin to take responsibility for the creation of a better, fuller existence for ourselves and finally accept that out of that creation we can build a better and more stable future. Whatever stage of understanding we may have reached, dreams can help and encourage us or indicate that we are going down a particular route that may not be worthwhile.

Dreams can be taken as events in their own right, and can be interpreted as such. Whether they make sense and whether we choose to act on the information must be decided by the dreamer. We can also accept dreams as an expression of the unconscious creative self, which can contain a message given either in an easy-to-understand form or in the language of symbolism, where initially the meanings are not easily discernible.

It is when we begin to recognize the creativity behind the process of dreaming that we open ourselves up to different ways of approaching our talents and abilities in a novel way. One of these is in the use of magic and the power to influence events.

THE HYPNAGOGIC AND HYPNOPOMPIC STATES

With practice, the states between waking and sleeping (or indeed sleeping and waking) can be a time when wishes and desires are given substance and brought into reality in a particularly magical way.

Briefly, the hypnagogic state occurs between waking and sleeping, while the hypnopompic occurs between sleeping and waking. The best explanation of these two states comes from the realm of spiritualism. The astral planes are levels of awareness that store the various thought-forms that have occurred, and in the hypnagogic and hypnopompic states the mind has some access to those realms, without actually seeing spirit form.

While dream interpretation itself does not necessarily require an understanding of the "hypno" states or vice versa, we can often use dream images and the hypno states to enhance our magical workings. The half-and-half awareness of consciousness

and the semi-dream state that we have in the hypnagogic state gives us an opportunity to follow a line of thought that can clear away problems in an almost magical way. Learning to use incantations, color, and symbolism in this state can be highly productive. One such incantation might be:

May the good I have done remain,
May the wrongs I have done be washed away.

At this time, when the mind is idling, a review of the day can lead to insights about our behavior or beliefs in surprising ways. By using this pre-sleep state to "download" each day's material, the mind can then bring forward deeper and more meaningful images in dreams, the understanding of which eventually allows us to take more control of our lives. We learn to dream magically and creatively rather than simply using dreams as a dumping ground. We then start the next day with a clean slate, and can use the hypnopompic state to bring order to the coming day.

This can be an exciting time, and may open up all sorts of possibilities, such as the exploration of telepathy, ESP (extra-sensory perception), healing, and so on. It is our choice as to which route of exploration we undertake.

By their very nature, flashes of ESP are symbolic and indistinct. When they occur spontaneously in the "hypno" states, they are more readily accepted as valid, and capable of interpretation in the same way as dream images. By becoming more practiced at working in that state, we become more able to use the magical and psychic senses if we wish. We are able to make use of a far more creative input than our "normal" awareness.

RELAXATION, MEDITATION AND VISUALIZATION

As aids to dreaming, the techniques of relaxation, meditation, and visualization are excellent. The more proficient you become in these techniques, the easier it is to attain creative dreaming. Some suggestions are included below:

Relaxation Technique

An easy relaxation technique that can be performed whether or not you use meditation, is as follows:

- Beginning with the toes, tighten and relax all the muscles in your body, so that you are able to identify the difference between tight and relaxed.
- Tighten each part of your body in turn.
- First tighten the toes and let go. Do this three times.
- Then tighten the ankles and release them. Again, repeat three times.
- Tighten the calves and let go. Again, repeat three times.
- Tighten the thighs and let go. Repeat twice more.
- Finally, tighten the full length of your legs completely and release, again repeating three times. (This exercise is good for restless leg syndrome.)
- Now move on to the rest of your body.

- Repeating three times for each part, tighten your buttocks, your stomach, your spine, your neck, your hands, your arms, and your neck (again), your face, and your scalp.

- Finally, tighten every single muscle you have used, and let go completely. Repeat three times. By now you should recognize the difference between the state of relaxation at the beginning of the exercise and the one at the end.

In time, with practice, you should be able to relax completely just by doing the last part of the exercise, but for now be content with taking yourself through the process slowly.

Meditation

One of the best ways of helping you dream and work magically is meditation. When you train yourself to recall material you need, and use personal symbolism, you improve your ability to concentrate and be aware. Practicing regularly brings many benefits. The aim in meditation is to keep the mind alert yet relaxed, and focused on a single subject rather than listening to the "chatterbox" in your head. A short period of meditation or creative visualization last thing at night gives you access to the full creative world of dreams, while a similar period in the morning allows you to work with and understand the dreams you have had.

Meditation Technique

First, choose a place where you will not be disturbed, and remember to silence phones and computers. To begin with, five minutes' meditation is enough.

- Sit upright in a chair or cross-legged on the floor with your back supported if necessary; it is important to be as comfortable as possible, although it is probably not a good idea to lie down, since you may fall asleep before the process of meditation is completed.

- Partially close your eyes to shut out the everyday world, or close your eyes completely. If you are an experienced meditator, you may find it easier to focus your attention on the bridge of your nose or the middle of your forehead.

- Breathe evenly and deeply; initially, breathe in for a count of four and out for a count of four. Once this rhythm is established, breathe out slightly longer than you breathe in, but at a rate that is still comfortable.

- Rather than being conscious of your breathing, become more aware of the breath itself. As you inhale, breathe in peace and tranquility; as you exhale, breathe out negativity. It should be possible to achieve a deep state of awareness. Any stray thoughts can be noted and dealt with later.

- At night, you may instruct yourself to remember any dreams that follow, or consider any problem you wish to solve. You may also use this period to creatively visualize something you desire, so it might be carried over into your dreams.

At this time, the best structure for doing a spell or ritual may present itself for consideration. Obviously, in the morning your concentration may be focused on the solution to your problem, the realization of your desires, or

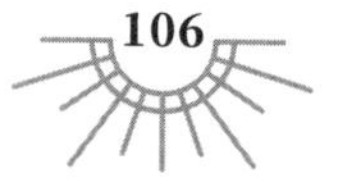

a magical technique that can help achieve the result you need. As you practice more, you may find that your period of meditation lasts up to twenty minutes. When you finish the meditation, try to keep your mind as clear as possible. Keep your physical movements unhurried, flowing in harmony with your tranquil state in preparation for magical working.

Dream Incubation

When we learn how to ask for guidance and help through dreams, or make life-changing decisions using magical means, we are becoming truly creative. This ties in with the belief that somewhere inside, there is a part of us that knows what is the best, or ideal, course of action. This aspect is called by some the Higher Self. Often we are not consciously aware of it, but giving ourselves permission to access it through dreams can have a profound effect on the way we manage our lives. Obviously the Higher Self can be used effectively for problem-solving, and for clarifying feelings we cannot otherwise handle. However, more importantly, working with dreams can give us ways of dealing with our fears and doubts. This leads to the positive use of power to enhance our natural abilities and talents. There is then the potential to obtain results in what often seems to be a magical way, as those interested in witchcraft do. If you would like to experiment with some spells, you can carry out the ones below safely to achieve the stated purpose.

To Drive Away Bad Dreams

This spell uses herbal magic and correspondences to clear the bedroom of negative influences. It is often a good idea to use material that is easily available, so you might use sprigs of rosemary, sage, lady's bedstraw, maize silks, or broom-corn. Since you want to have something taken away, you should perform this magical working as the Moon wanes.

YOU WILL NEED

- Bowl of warm water
- Salt
- Sprigs of herbs
- String

METHOD

- Dissolve the salt in the warm water.
- Tie the herbs together.
- Dip the sprigs in the water and sprinkle the corners of the room with the water.
- Use the sprigs to sprinkle the saltwater on your bedclothes, particularly around the head and foot of the bed.

- When you have done this, place the herbs under your pillow, or if you prefer, under the middle of the bed.

- The next morning, discard the herbs at a crossroads if you can, by either burying them or allowing them to disperse to the four winds. Otherwise, ensure that you have carried them away from your home.

- This carries all negativity away from your bedroom and bed.

This spell uses rosemary, which brings clarity, sage for wisdom, lady's bedstraw, which is said to have lined the manger at Christ's birth, and broom corn, which is used in worship of the Mexican goddess Chicomecohuatl. All of these herbs bring cleansing not just of the room but also of the occupant's aura or subtle energy. On the basis that one should always replace negative with positive, you may like to use the following technique to bring about positive dreams.

Having prepared your environment, this technique is most useful when there is a strong, deeply felt association with the issue or request being considered—in magical terms, ideal conditions for spell working. It is like being able to consult an encyclopedia that contains a wealth of information—in fact, the Higher Self.

Asking for the Dreams You Want

This may work most effectively for those who have already learned how to recall and record their dreams, as shown below. These methods have already established the lines of communication, but it also works well for those who have learned to meditate, or who use other kinds of self-management tools, such as creative visualization or chanting. The technique is a very easy one, particularly if you have learned through work or other experience to remain focused on issues at hand.

Use as a memory jogger the word "CARDS," which stands for the following points:

- Clarify the issue

- Ask the question

- Repeat it

- Dream and document it

- Study the dream

"C" means that you spend time clarifying what the issue is. When you identify the basic aspects of what seems to be blocking your progress, or where you are stuck, you can gain some insight into your mental processes. You have thus laid the groundwork.

Try to state the issue as positively as you can; for example, "Promotions pass me by," rather than "I'm not getting promoted." The subconscious tends to latch on to negative statements rather than positive, so if you state the problem negatively you are allowing negative energy to gain a foothold. Don't try to resolve the situation at that point.

"A" suggests that you ask the appropriate question using an old journalistic technique: Who? What? Where? When? Why? Then figure out what the relevant question is. For instance, in our example, you might ask:

Who can help me get a promotion? What must

I do to be in line for a promotion? Where do the best opportunities lie for me? When will I be able to use my greater experience? Why is my expertise not being recognized?

You can see that all these questions are open questions, and are not necessarily tied to any time frame. They allow you to decide where your knowledge of magical influence or spell making is best applied. If you ask a confused question, you may get a confusing answer, so try to get as close to the heart of the matter as you can. Conversely, by asking inappropriate questions, you may get answers you don't want.

Repeat the question. Just as restating an incantation builds up power, by repeating the question over and over you are fixing it in the subconscious. Blocks of three often work well, so repeating three sets of three (nine times in all) means that it should have reached deep into your unconscious.

As you compose yourself for sleep and use your relaxation techniques, tell yourself that you will have a dream that will give you an answer to your question or problem. Dream command means informing your inner self that you will have a dream that will help. If you wish, as you repeat the question, tap lightly on your third eye in the center of your forehead.

A word of warning: the dreaming self is quite wayward, so to begin with you may not receive an answer on the night you request it. You may only receive part of an answer, or nothing for several nights, and then a series of dreams that tell you what you need to know. It is a highly individual process, and no one can tell you how it should be. With time, you will recognize your own pattern, but be prepared to be patient.

Dream it. When you do dream, document it briefly as soon as you can, noting down the main theme and anything else you think might help you in your magical practice.

Study the dream in more detail when you have time to do so. Look carefully at the imagery in the dream, which will probably be fairly straightforward. Look for details, clues, and hidden meanings, see whether you can apply any of them to situations in your everyday life, and use your knowledge of symbolism to help you decide whether developing a spell or ritual will make your life more fulfilling or easier to handle. Sometimes a suggestion for a new way of acting, or the answer to a question, can come from applying the information to a different part of your life, before you get around to tackling the question you have asked.

As you become more proficient at dealing with the information that becomes available to you, you may find that the nature of your questions changes and becomes more proactive. For instance, you may find yourself asking, "How can I make __ happen?" or "What if I did ___?" This is true creativity, and gives you the opportunity to practice your spell making and magic in different ways. It is the exciting process of the appearance of the magical "you" appearing in your external life.

A Dream Journal

Keeping a dream journal—that is, recording every one of the dreams you can recall—can be a fascinating but difficult task. Over a period of time, while it can give you information from all sorts of angles, it is an extremely efficient tool in prophetic dreaming.

You may find that you go through a period when most or all of your dreams seem to be around a particular theme—for instance, that

of the Gods and Goddesses. Thinking that you have understood those dreams, you can explore the theme in waking life and enhance your knowledge.

It can be interesting to discover months, or perhaps years, later that the same pattern and theme recurs, with additional information and clarity. By keeping a dream journal at the same time as recording the methods and results of your magical spells or meditations, you can chart your progress in becoming adept at divination dreaming.

The dreaming self is highly efficient in that it will present information in different ways until you get the message. Equally, that same dreaming self can be inefficient in that the information can be shrouded in extraneous material and symbolism that will need to be sorted out of the rubble. It's up to you to decide which explanation is relevant, so if you are using your dreams as a magical tool, you will interpret them in that light.

A dream journal allows you to assess not just the content of your dreams, but also the pattern of your dreaming. Many people are highly prolific dreamers, others less so, and many more have what could be called "big" dreams rarely. In fact, we all dream at some point, every night, often without remembering, although it does appear that the more we learn to remember our dreams the more proficient we become at dreaming. It is as though the more we use the "muscle," the better it responds.

Keeping a Dream Journal

- Any paper and writing instrument can be used—whatever is most pleasing to you, though it can add extra power if you have prepared your journal and implements specially. You could prepare them according to the technique for magical writing.

- Keep your paper and pens handy. You could also use your phone's Voice Memo function to record your dreams. "Speaking" the dream fixes it in your mind, enabling you to be in touch with the feelings and emotions of the dream. It is sometimes easier to explain the dream in the present tense. For instance, "I'm standing on a hill," rather than, "I was standing on a hill."

- Write the account of the dream as soon as possible after waking. Not everyone is interested in analyzing their dreams, but keeping an account of your more inexplicable or "way-out" dreams is helpful.

- Use as much detail as possible. A hastily scribbled dream is harder to decipher than one that goes into more detail.

- Be consistent in how you record your dreams. One simple scheme is given below.

- If you are learning how to use your dreams magically, make a note of when you realize you are dreaming.

Recording Your Dreams

This technique is an easy way for you to record your dreams. Obviously, the first three parts only need to be recorded if you intend to submit your dream to an outside source. If you intend to keep your dream journal private, this method gives you the opportunity to look at each of your dreams and return to them later, perhaps to compare content, scenarios, or other aspects. It can also allow you to quantify your progress in the art of self-development.

- Name
- Age
- Gender
- Date of dream
- Where were you when you recalled the dream?
- State the content of the dream
- Write down anything odd about the dream (e.g. animals, bizarre situations, etc.)
- What were your feelings in/about the dream?

DREAM MANAGEMENT

If you are just beginning to record your dreams, the important thing is not to try too hard. Being relaxed about the whole thing will give far more potential for success than getting worked up because you can't remember your dream or you don't appear to have dreamed at all. The more you practice, the easier it becomes.

If you decide to keep a dream journal, it is worthwhile incorporating it into the preparation for sleep. By making these preparations into a ritual, it can help concentrate your mind on the activity of dreaming, and thinking over a situation before you go to sleep. Meditating on it can help open the doors of the unconscious to some of the answers you are seeking.

Carefully laying out your tools, rereading some old dreams, using deep relaxation methods assisted by relaxing oils or herbal teas, and even asking the super-conscious for usable material can assist in the creative dreaming process.

Sleep

In myth, Hypnos, the god of sleep, was usually personified in winged form as one of the inevitable forces of nature. He is always pictured as young and fair, although some say he was the father of Morpheus, the god of dreams. A sip from Hypnos' cup or a touch from his staff is said by some to send you into blissful sleep until his mother, Nyx (Night), has fled the sky.

YOU WILL NEED

- Cup of herbal tea, such as chamomile
- Dream journal
- Pen
- Crystal, such as diaspor or jade

METHOD

Hold the cup in both hands and say:

Hypnos, Lord of Sleep, son of Night Bless this cup and give me rest

That I may benefit from all your might And know forever what is best

- Drink from the cup.

- Put the journal and the pen together close to your bed with the crystal on top.

Say:

Morpheus Morpheus, shaper of dreams
Crafter of light not all that it seems
Send me now, images fit only for kings
Those that fulfill my deepest yearnings
Let me remember all that I learn
True to myself, to you I now turn

- Now compose yourself for sleep and await developments.

Morpheus had special responsibility for the dreams of kings and heroes, and gave shape to those beings who inhabit dreams. He is petitioned here in the knowledge that you are a monarch of all you survey and that your journal will help you understand.

On Waking

In the morning, try to wake up naturally, without an alarm clock. There are devices on the market, such as daylight simulators that come on gradually, dimmer switches, and clocks that have a soft alarm, graduating in intensity. Even a radio or tape recorder programmed to play soft, relaxing music can be used. Using such waking aids can help you hold on to the hypnagogic state and use it creatively. Some dreamers have reported that the spoken word seems to chase away a dream.

On waking, lie as still as possible for a moment, and try to recall what you have dreamed. Often it is the most startling thing or feeling that you will remember first, followed by lesser elements. Write these elements in your journal, and write the "story" of the dream. This may give you an initial perception that is sufficient for your needs, both in the everyday and from a magical perspective. Sometimes much can be gained from taking the dream action forward using the questions, "What happens next?" or "What if?" Let us assume that your dream was about an argument with someone who is close to you in waking life. You wake with the situation unresolved, but are aware that this suggests some inner conflict. Try to imagine what would happen if the argument continued. Would you or your opponent "win"? What if your opponent won? How would you feel? What if you won?

Working Creatively with Dreams

When you have been recording your dreams for a while, you may find it useful to turn one of them into a creative project. This could be a painting, sculpture, or other artistic process. It could also be a short story, perhaps taking the dream further forward, a play, or even using nature creatively—it needs to be something that takes one beyond normal activities. Look particularly for magical and fantasy aspects, because you are trying to access the world of magic in a slightly different way from that of ordinary spell making and ritual.

By acknowledging the creative processes in dreams and making them tangible in reality, you are opening yourself up to all sorts of possibilities and changes of consciousness. One of the benefits of deliberately dreaming creatively is a different perception of events in

the world around you. Colors may appear more vibrant, shapes sharper, and sounds clearer. These changes can be quite subtle, but they usually bring more focus to your awareness and allow you to use creativity to your advantage in small things as well as more important ones. Life begins to take on new meaning.

Dream symbols, because they are archetypal and tap into a wider consciousness than your own, are fertile ground for meditation, which can allow unconscious insights to come to the surface, giving rise to even greater creativity. You may wish to meditate on the overall feeling or one particular aspect of the dream. When you find yourself dreaming about your chosen project, you have come full circle—from an acorn to an oak tree and back to an acorn—akin to rebirth.

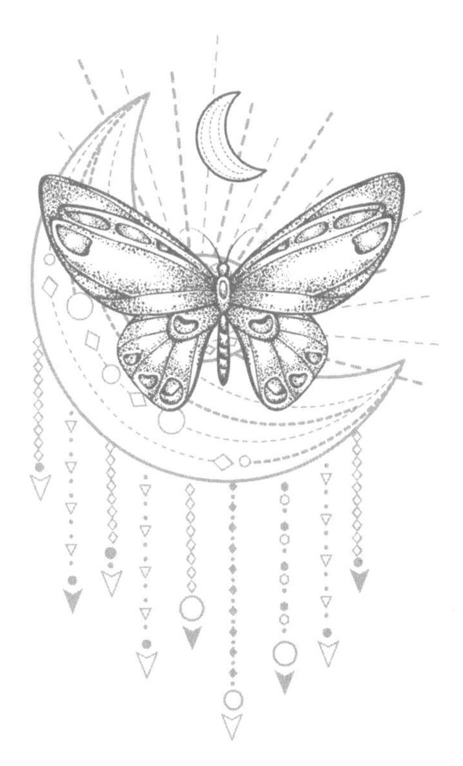

It does not matter whether the project is good or bad; what's important is the enjoyment you get from it. One of the most fulfilling aspects of such a process is the realization that you have entered a stream of consciousness that belongs to all of us, but which so few manage to tap into. This "locking on" can give a strong physical sensation as much as an emotional or spiritual one. The counter-balance to this is the number of times that you will get stuck or come up against a brick wall in this part of the process, but perseverance brings about a greater understanding of your inner, more magical, self.

For the purposes of self-development, you may like to keep a separate journal or record of the processes and stages of awareness experienced during this strenuous activity—it is worthwhile to spend a short time each day working with your project, and a journal allows you to see how far you have traveled in this journey of discovery. It can be fascinating to see, for instance, in looking back over your daybook, how you have found it easier to recognize when the fears and doubts arise, and how you have dealt with them.

It may be that your creative journal takes precedence over the dream one, or vice versa. It is possible that, with time, you will recognize that your dreams change when you are in a more overtly creative phase. You may be able to clear a creative block by asking your dreams for an answer or by using the in-between states. You will gradually find that you will be able to intertwine the various states of awareness when necessary without losing the reality of each one. This is the true use of dream creativity.

DREAM SPELLS AND TECHNIQUES

To have the courage to transcend fears, doubts, and barriers we encounter in becoming creative and working magically, we need to be in touch with our "inner being" and the creative urge that is ours by right. We must move from feeling that we are prevented by circumstances from being the person we know we can be to taking control of our lives and being able to link to that stream of knowledge and awareness that enables us to predict and, more importantly, create our future.

To do this, we have to be practical. To that end, this section contains exercises, tips, and techniques that will help you develop creative dreaming. You do not necessarily need to follow the order below, although this is the one that is probably the simplest, because it takes you from when you first remember and record your dreams to using them with full awareness.

Dreaming with intent is such an integral part of magical working and spell making that it is worthwhile to take the time to develop the art to help you to enhance conscious spell making, and also to enable you to use dreaming itself as a magical tool.

Work Plan

Dreamwork can be defined as any activity that you carry out once you have had a dream. It entails working initially only with the content of a particular dream. Later it can be investigated along with other dreams, to see whether it is part of a series or perhaps clarifies other previous dreams. The dream can be looked at in several different ways. You should be able to:

- List all the components.
- Explore the symbols with all their shades of meanings.
- Widen the perspectives and components.
- Work with the dream in as many different ways as possible to complete unfinished business.
- Work with the spiritual significances.
- Bring the message through to everyday life to make necessary choices and changes.

The Components

The components of a dream are the various parts: the scenario, the people, the action, the feelings and emotions. Each has its role to play in your interpretation, and it is only when you consider the dream carefully that you will be able to appreciate the more subtle meanings. In lucid or creative dreaming, it is feasible to make changes to any or all of these things, though not necessarily all at once.

The more adept you become at recognizing your own way of creating your dreams, the easier your interpretation will be. Making a simple list will help you do this.

Psychologists Calvin Hall and Robert van de Castle, in an effort to be scientific, developed the method of quantitative coding that is still used in dream research. This led to the cognitive theory of dreams, which meant that dream content was divided into several categories. There were characters, emotions, interactions, misfortunes, objects, and settings. By dividing dreams in this way, they recognized that these expressed the way we see our family members, friends, social environment, and self. Dreams reflect waking concerns, interests, and emotional focus. When carrying out their research, they discovered that there were strong similarities in the dreams of people all over the world.

The Symbols

When the mind has a message to impart, it will often present the information in symbolic form. It is important, therefore, for you to understand the symbolism of your dreams. Over time, you will develop your own symbolism. Certain things will have meaning for you. The conventional symbolism of dreams is very rich in imagery.

Particularly in magical work, it is worthwhile to take a thorough look at your dreams, so any symbols can be properly interpreted. Any good dream-interpretation book will act as a starting point. With any of your dreams, it is useful to make an alphabetical list of their content and then decide whether it can be interpreted symbolically rather than literally.

The Perspectives

Perhaps the most satisfactory dreamwork is deliberately to widen the perspective in the dream and consciously push it further. Thus, you might like to see what would happen next to one of the characters. For example, what would happen if the action continued? How would the other characters react? How would this change the dream? If a particular character acted in a different manner, would the whole dream change, or only parts of it? How much would you want characters to support you or leave you alone? You can see that these considerations mark the beginning of you taking control in the dream, and you are therefore moving more authoritatively into dreaming magically. Another way in which you can change perspective is to look at your dream as if you were one of the characters. If this were so, would you "direct" the dream differently? Would there be a different outcome? Working with your dream in this way enables you to become more aware of the effect on various parts of your personality (the characters in your dream).

Working with Your Dreams

You can use any approach you are comfortable with to look at issues connected with your dreams. You might like to use either the Jungian method of working or some of those mentioned above. The Jungian method recognizes the archetypes (basic constructs) as important elements of everyone's personality. It is these that give us myths and fairy tales.

Working with the Spiritual Significances

From the idea that God, as seen in ancient societies, gives dreams, we would now speak of a recognition of spiritual influences. This is when your altruistic side recognizes that you must make adjustments to your behavior if you are to live your life as fully as possible. Magical working takes on new meaning when your intuition informs your everyday spell making.

By and large, the spiritual significance of a dream has to do with your sense of responsibility to the rest of your community or the world. If a dream does not allow itself to be interpreted in any other way, you may wish to interpret it from the perspective of the Greater Good—that which benefits mankind rather than just the individual. The three things to look for here are right thought, right speech, and right action. The questions you might ask yourself are:

- How does this dream help me be a better person?
- What information does it give me to help others?
- What fresh understanding does this dream bring me?

Bringing the Message Through

Once you have learned to explore your dreams, you will be able to practice new patterns of behavior, think in new ways, change some attitudes, and create a new way of being. As time goes on, you will find that you can, in the dream state, practice your new mode of behavior before making radical changes in your everyday life. You should also be able to get an idea of the effect your behavior will have on other people.

In this section you will find various techniques and spells for expanding your dreams and learning how to work magically through them. If you are going to use your dreams to help you deal with your everyday life, there are certain techniques that you must practice first, to clear your mind so you can work perceptively and honestly with magical energies.

As part of your nightly routine to clear your mind for dreaming, and later for magical working, it is wise to do what might be called a daily audit. This consists of doing a review of your day and balancing the good with the bad. You might like to concentrate on your behavior and decide whether you have acted appropriately, or decide which actions have been productive and which have not. Your audit will look at the issues that concern you. Your starting point should be the hour immediately preceding bedtime—then work backwards throughout the day until you reach your time of awakening.

- Take a sheet of paper and divide it into two columns. On one side list actions and types of behavior you consider good, and on the other those you consider bad or indifferent.
- Looking at the bad side first, review where your behavior or action could be improved and resolve to do better in the future. You may like to develop a technique for yourself that represents your rejection of disliked behaviors. This can be as simple as writing down the behavior and discarding the paper on which it is written; or, you may use the Bay Leaves spell below.
- Now look at the good side and give yourself approval and encouragement. Resolve to practice more of the good behavior and, if you wish, find an affirmation that indicates this.
- Where your behavior has been indifferent, resolve to do better and give yourself more positive feedback for having made the effort.
- Forgive yourself for not having achieved perfection and praise yourself for doing your best. This is the aspect of "balancing your books." Now let your day go, do not dwell on the negatives, and go peacefully to sleep. This exercise helps keep you spiritually strong and clear in your purpose.

Bay Leaves Spell

This spell uses plant magic and fire to achieve its purpose. The bay leaf possesses powerful magical properties. The first part is best done at the time of the New Moon, and the result will often have come to pass by the time of the Full Moon.

YOU WILL NEED

- 3 bay leaves
- Paper or parchment
- Pen
- Candle

METHOD

- Write down your intent to change your behavior three times on the paper, repeating the wish aloud.
- Place the bay leaves on the paper. Fold the paper into thirds and visualize your wish coming true. Fold the paper into thirds again and hide it in a dark place. Keep visualizing your behavior changing as you do this.
- Once you are satisfied with your new behavior, light the candle and burn the paper as a thank-you. Allow the candle to burn out.

Bay promotes wisdom and protects you from making mistakes. This spell is obviously best done in private. You should never reveal your intent to others, so be clear that the intent is for the Greater Good.

Remembering Your Dreams

To remember your dreams and use them as magical tools, you need to train yourself to

remember most of their content. Good-quality sleep is the first prerequisite since, while you are training yourself, you may find that you wake up fairly frequently. Later you will be able to remember both small and important dreams, but first you must get into a particular routine.

- If you have an illness or are taking medication, please check with your doctor or medical practitioner before undertaking this exercise.
- Decide which sleep periods you are going to monitor. A good idea is to give yourself an approximate four-hour period for sleep, then monitor everything after that.

- Set your alarm or wake-up device—preferably soft light or soothing music—for the time you wish to wake. Under no circumstances allow yourself to be "shocked" into wakefulness, for example with loud music. It's counterproductive because it is likely to chase away the dream.
- When you have woken up, lie perfectly still. Do not move until you have recalled your dream in as much detail as possible.
- Write down your dream, including as much information as you can, and work with it—for instance, noting symbols or ideas for magical working—when you are ready to do so.
- It is here that your dream journal will come in handy, because in it you will also be able to record fragments of dreams that at the time may not seem relevant, but might later on.
- Dreams are thought to be remembered best from periods of Rapid Eye Movement sleep, so with practice you should begin to discover when these periods are. Don't be too worried if at first your dream recall seems to be deficient. You will get better each time with practice.
- Try not to let the affairs of the day get in the way when you first wake up. You can begin to consider them when you have taken notice of your mind's nighttime activity.

How to Have a "Magical" Dream

This technique is extremely simple and is a potent tool in dealing with our internal gremlins. More importantly, it is a way of raising our consciousness and developing our ability to access our creative, magical minds. However, unless you hit upon it involuntarily, this is a technique that needs some training. Try not to be disappointed in the results you achieve at first; you will improve if you have patience.

1. Prepare Yourself for Sleep

As you prepare yourself for sleep, give yourself the instruction that tonight you will have a creative or magical dream. Form an affirmation of intent along the lines of a simple statement such as, "Tonight my dream will be magical." Keep the statement simple, because you are learning to open your mind to possibilities. The content of the dream does not matter.

2. Repeat Your Affirmation

Repeat your affirmation, either out loud or to yourself, as many times as you need to in order to fix it in your mind. This teaches you to focus your mind on one thing at a time. An affirmation is a simple, positive statement encapsulating as succinctly as possible what you want to happen.

3. Hold Your Intent in Mind

Keep your mind on your intention, then allow yourself to drift off to sleep.

4. Note Your Degree of Awareness

When you wake up, note the time and whether you were an observer or a participant in your dream. Also note how long you think you were in that state of awareness. Your estimation will probably not be very accurate to begin with, but that doesn't matter, since you will become more proficient as time goes on.

Incubating a Specific Magical Dream

When you have had some success with incubating (creating or growing) the type of dream you want using the CARDS method, you can progress to developing a specific magical dream. Be patient; at first you might not get the exact environment or content you want. Gradually, however, you will find that you are hitting your target more often.

Practice this technique at times when you know you will be able to use the information, record it, or carry out research to resolve any doubts that may need further explanation.

1. Prepare the Focus of Your Dream

This might be to understand a ritual, discover the correct incense or herb to use, or even develop a new spell. Before you go to bed, take the time to narrow your thoughts down to a single idea or query that clearly states the subject of your concern. Remember that although you are focusing on a single idea, you are also seeking the widest—or perhaps most important—information you can access, so this may manifest in more than one dream.

Write your idea or query down and use a visual image, such as a picture or appropriate symbol, to fix the idea in your mind. Memorize the idea and the visual image. Try to incorporate a trigger word, sound, or symbol that alerts you to a deeper state of awareness. Remind yourself that when you dream of that trigger, you will know you're dreaming. Repeat to yourself at least three times, "When I dream of ____, I will remember that I am dreaming."

2. Go to Bed

It's important not to let anything intrude on your concentration. So, without further ado, go to bed and make yourself comfortable.

3. Keep the Phrase or Image in Your Mind

Concentrate on your phrase and image and deepen your awareness. Imagine yourself already dreaming about your query. As you become more proficient at controlling your dreams, if there is something you want to experiment with in the dream, such as flying, concentrate on the idea of being in full control.

4. Meditate on the Phrase

Keep your objective in focus until you fall asleep. If at all possible, don't let any other thoughts come between thinking about your issue and falling asleep. If your thoughts wander, just revert to thinking about your phrase and its magical significance.

5. Follow Your Focus

When you have begun dreaming, try to be extra- aware of matters pertaining to the issue at hand. Do not try to take control of your dream, since you are allowing your unconscious self—that part that is in contact with all magical and other knowledge—to "speak" to you through the dream. Accept that symbols and information will appear that can be figured out afterwards, and allow the dream to reach its fulfillment. Note your impressions and be aware of as much of the content of the dream as you can.

6. Keep the Dream Active, and Sustain It If You Can

Remember that magical information has a language all its own and often needs interpreting in more than one way. While you do not need to take control of the dream, you do need to trust your intuition to be aware of how much information it can assimilate. For this reason, you should learn that it is possible to go back into a dream in order to highlight issues that have not been fully understood.

7. Returning to the Everyday

As you wake up, try to remain for a time in the hypnopompic (half-awake) state and learn to check whether you feel you have received adequate information in order to proceed. Finally, rouse yourself to full consciousness, and get ready to record everything you've learned.

8. Record the Dream

Record the dream as shown previously, deciding how it has answered your question or intent.

Analyzing Your Dream

You will want to get into the habit of analyzing the content of your dreams more fully for magical significances. A simple way to do this is to divide it into segments so that you can consider each part of the dream and whether it had any relevance to your magical workings. For instance, dreaming of one of the gods or goddesses might alert you to the whole realm of their rulership of herbs, crystals, and other magical necessities. The main theme of the dream may open up a number of other possibilities that you have not previously considered.

Make the following headings under which to analyze your dream:

- The dream.
- The dream segments.
- The differences/similarities in the segments.
- The main theme of the dream.

ADVANCED TECHNIQUES

Now, having practiced the basic techniques for magical dreaming, you are ready to move on to the more advanced methods. Before you do that, however, take time to consolidate what you have learned. Think carefully about what you have been doing and whether you are satisfied with the results. Is there anything you could do to improve your methods?

- Do you want to try anything else?
- What do you want to happen now?
- How do you want to use magical dreaming in the future?
- Do you need to do further research?
- Do you want to put yourself in touch with other people who are practicing magical dreaming?

The more advanced techniques help you focus on your objectives and decide whether you are more interested in researching the technique or whether you want to be creative and help make things happen.

It often helps to alter the way you express yourself to accommodate the creativity of dreams. If your day-to-day self-expression takes place with words, then experiment with color or form. If you enjoy music, try to find a particular piece that expresses the mood of your dream. If you are a sedentary person, express elements of the dream through movement such as dance or Eastern disciplines of t'ai chi or qi gung. The basic idea is that you can use your dreams to enhance your creativity in everyday life. They can act as starting points for projects or they can be used to explore other modes of self-expression.

Directing Your Dreams

This technique is a way of achieving changes of a mystical kind. Learning the technique helps consolidate the idea of being able to create magical changes in your environment. At this stage, it is more a matter of actually changing the environment in which your dream takes place. Remember that you can do anything you please in the dream state, and later you may be able to effect change in your everyday life. This is an extension of creative visualization. You can use the idea of the "big screen" or of a stage production. Begin with a remembered dream. Start by changing something small in it and gradually work up to bigger changes.

- Replay the dream and do everything at different speeds. Play with what you are creating, using your imagination to manipulate the dream reality. It is important to have fun with this since you are deliberately operating your creative ability.
- You might then like to think of yourself as the

director and producer of your own play. You can use any props you like and experiment to achieve the right atmosphere.

- Follow this up by creating a stage set for your next learning experience.

Recognize that you are creating a reality that has many possibilities, but you have the power to choose yours.

The IFE Technique

Life teaches us that we need restrictions. From an early age, we learn what is acceptable behavior and what is not. On the whole, we are taught that to be spontaneous is dangerous, and we must be "sensible." Within the framework of creativity and magical dreams, however, we have the freedom to be totally eccentric and to use patterns of behavior that re-educate us in the art of personal freedom.

Most creative people have a highly developed ability to create fantasies. If you dare to take spell making to its limits, you will find that you are capable of doing and being things that are not possible except in an altered state of consciousness, just as the magicians of old used to do. Shape-shifting is one example of this.

One yoga exercise that is designed to give a sense of the meaning of life is to try to discover what it is like to be a tree or flower or an otherwise sentient (aware) being. This exercise consists of three stages, which here we call the IFE Technique.

- Imagine what it would be like to be your chosen object.

- Feel how the object feels. Experience being that object. Because the rational aspects of everyday life are suspended during creative dreams and magical working, you should quickly be able to reach a state of awareness where it is easy to do all these things. You could practice being the opposite sex, being an animal—domesticated or otherwise—or, if you are feeling brave, a rock or the sea. Initially you will probably not be able to hold this state for long, but with practice you will find that it becomes easier, and that you can widen your perception to encompass other states of being. You might, for instance, try to experience what it would be like to be suspended in space or time, to belong to other worlds or even to sense what you will be like in 20 years.

When you are relaxed, it is also possible to use other techniques to help you in the art of magical working.

- A simple way of preparing for creative dreaming and magical working is to use contemplation. In this, as a precursor to meditation, you give yourself a visual image of the subject at hand.

- You might, for instance, think of the words "spell making" carved out of a block of wood. Holding this image in your mind, let it develop and watch what happens.

- You might wish to consider the idea of a visit to Egypt or some other far-flung country to enhance your magical workings, so again you hold the idea in your mind and contemplate it. This might lead to the opportunity for an actual visit or a dream that clarifies an issue for you.

- When you have become proficient at contemplation, you can attempt meditation, which is a further stage of allowing an image or thought to develop spontaneously. You may then wish to take the results of your meditation back into creative dreaming and magical working.

Crystals

Many people believe that working with crystals can enhance dreaming and help us access the wisdom in these natural objects. It is as though the subtle energies act as both receivers and transmitters, and allow us to tune into those aspects of knowledge in ourselves and our world.

Most good crystal or New Age shops have a good selection of stones and their meanings. It is easy to program your crystals to help you in your dream work.

UNDERSTANDING ARCHETYPAL IMAGES

Archetypal images are basic concepts, patterns, and symbols that are hidden in the collective unconscious until we choose to activate them. They appear in dreams, mythology, and fairy tales, and are a rich source of imagery in magical working.

Myths, Astrological Planets and Numbers

1. Choose a particular trigger—a myth, planet, or number—and think about how the story, or the qualities, might apply to your life.
2. Contemplate the story or qualities, and feel how powerful they are. Here you are preparing to use both imagination and visualization.
3. Put yourself in the position you wish to be in, that is, as a character in the myth, on a planet, or expressing its qualities. Imagine what it would be like to be part of that scenario. If working with numbers, think of the qualities of that number and sense them inside you (see pages 60-69).
4. You might like to use your sense of shape—a square, a pentagram, and so on—to explore its qualities. A pentagram will feel different from a square, and this is exploring the meaning of numbers and shape. Gradually, you should become aware of the qualities of each shape and progress to a more solid shape.
5. Try testing the boundaries of that shape, and move the figure to be larger or smaller. Play with the shape in any way you like. Make

it into a solid object and try to find out what it would be like to be inside such an object.
6. Allow yourself to go to sleep, and remember that with enhanced awareness you can do anything you choose. Dreams triggered by myths, planets, archetypal images, and so forth will have a far deeper content than "ordinary" dreams. They are a rich library of magical knowledge.

Focused Reverie

By the time you have begun to make your dreams work for you, you are in a position to manipulate your dreams even further. Almost inevitably we come up against the question of whether the technique about to be described is lucid dreaming. While it is described here as focused reverie, its name really does not matter. The technique is to remember the dream up to the time when you wake up, then consciously choose to take the dream as a whole forward.

It has already been suggested that you might work with characters and objects in your dream. This method can be extended to include the whole dream, and simply allows the dream to continue in its own way. The steps to achieve this are quite simple:

1. Remembering the dream as it was, make contact with each part of the dream as though it were still happening.
2. Now put yourself in the position of observer and allow the dream to unfold around you.
3. Do not attempt to influence the dream. Just allow it to happen.
4. If the action or characters get stuck, assume that is the point at which you would have woken up.
5. Think about why the dream will not go any further. Resolve to deal with any issues that arise.
6. You might choose to influence your future dreams in light of what you discover.

This technique is, in effect, a kind of meditation or waking dream, and unites the dream state with the ordinary everyday world.

To Make a Dream Pillow

Dream pillows may be used for several purposes. You can use them to enhance sleep, in which case any of the following six herbs may be used: catnip, hops, lavender, thyme, valerian, or vervain (to prevent nightmares).

YOU WILL NEED

- 1 part each of at least five dried herbs from those listed above
- Bowl
- Dried orange and lemon peel
- 1/2 part mugwort
- 1 part myrrh or frankincense resin
- 2 pieces of lightweight fabric such as muslin
- Needle and thread
- Your choice of decoration, e.g. ribbon, buttons

METHOD

- Burn a little frankincense or myrrh resin to cleanse your working area.

- Mix the five dried herbs in the bowl in whatever proportion feels right. While doing this, think about the purpose of your dream pillow; for example, hops will give a sound sleep, mugwort induces psychic dreaming, and chamomile promotes a feeling of well-being.

- Crumble the dried peels into small pieces and add the rest of the finely ground resin to this mixture.

- Sew together three sides of the fabric, leaving one side open so you can add the herbs. Make a mental link with Hypnos, the Greek god of sleep, or Demeter, Earth Mother.

- Decorate the bag with symbols of your choosing. Fill the pillow (not too full) with the herb and resin mixture and sew up the final side.

- You may use your dream pillow whenever you like. Slip it into your pillowcase and inhale.

Dream pillows are useful if, for instance, you are away from home and want to create a certain ambience, or if you need continuity while working on a dream project.

A Spell for While You Sleep

Knot magic has a the effect of binding or fixing a spell in place, and with the addition of color it is possible to use ribbons to bring about a desired outcome. You can use the colors you associate with different ideas, for example, green with money and prosperity, red with love, and yellow with health. Go with the color correspondence that makes sense to you. By using your bed as a focus, your magical work can be done while you sleep. This is a personal way of working, and one that can bring particularly positive results.

YOU WILL NEED

- Four lengths of colored ribbon that can be tied easily
- Four pins
- Your bed

METHOD

- If your bed has bedposts, simply knot a length of the colored ribbon for your purpose around each post.

- Each time you do this, say:

With this knot of colored ribbon
Bring to me the power hidden.
Grant me that right
Throughout this night.

- If your bed has no posts, pin the knotted ribbon to each corner using the same words.

- Each night for two nights, touch each ribbon knot in turn and repeat the words above.

- Leave the ribbons in place until you no longer feel the need for them.

You can expect to have some fairly vivid dreams over the following three nights, which may help you develop the qualities you seek. This spell allows your unconscious self to work in a protected space without the chatter of day-to-day matters.

Further reading

TEA-LEAF READING

Tea Leaf Reading by Dennis Fairchild

The Art of Tea Leaf Reading by Jane Struthers

The Cup of Destiny by Jane Lyle

CRYSTAL DIVINATION

Cassandra Eason's Healing Crystals

The Crystal Bible by Judy Hall

Crystal Healing Essentials by Cassandra Eason

Crystals, How to Use Crystal Energy to Enhance Your Life by Judy Hall

Crystal Prescriptions Volume 3 by Judy Hall

The Complete Guide to Manifesting With Crystals by Marina Costello

Essential Book of Crystals by Emily Anderson

CHINESE ASTROLOGY

Unveil Your Destiny by Vincent Koh

The Definitive Book of Chinese Astrology by Shelly Wu

Secrets of Your Birth Chart by Lillian Too

The Destiny Code by Joey Yap

I CHING

I Ching by Hilary Barrett

I Ching by Daniel Bernardo

The I Ching for Romance and Friendship by Rosemary Burr

NUMEROLOGY

The Ultimate Guide to Numerology by Tania Gabrielle

Numerology with Tantra, Ayurveda and Astrology by Harish Johari

PALMISTRY

The Hand in Psychological Diagnosis by Charlotte Wolff

The Book of the Hand by Fred Gettings

The Book of Palmistry by Fred Gettings

Your Life in Your Hands by Beryl Hutchinson

Palmistry 4 Today by Frank Clifford

Dermatoglyphics in Medical Disorders by Schauman & Alter

Your Palm, Barometer of Health by David Brandon-Jones

Palmistry – Your Career in Your Hands by Andrew Fitzherbert & Nathaniel Altman

Medical Palmistry – A Doctor's Guide to Better Health through Hand Analysis by Dr. Eugene Scheimann & Nathaniel Altman

The Nail in Clinical Diagnosis by Beaven & Brooks

Hand Psychology by Andrew Fitzherbert

The Spellbinding Power of Palmistry by Johnny Fincham

RUNES

Nordic Runes by Paul Rhys Mountfort

Futhark: A Handbook of Rune Magic by Edred Thorsson

The Book of Seidr by Runic John

PROPHETIC DREAMING

The Seer by James W. Goll

Prophetic Visions and Dreams by Les D. Crause

10,000 Dreams Interpreted by Pamela Ball